BRAND LIKE A GIRL

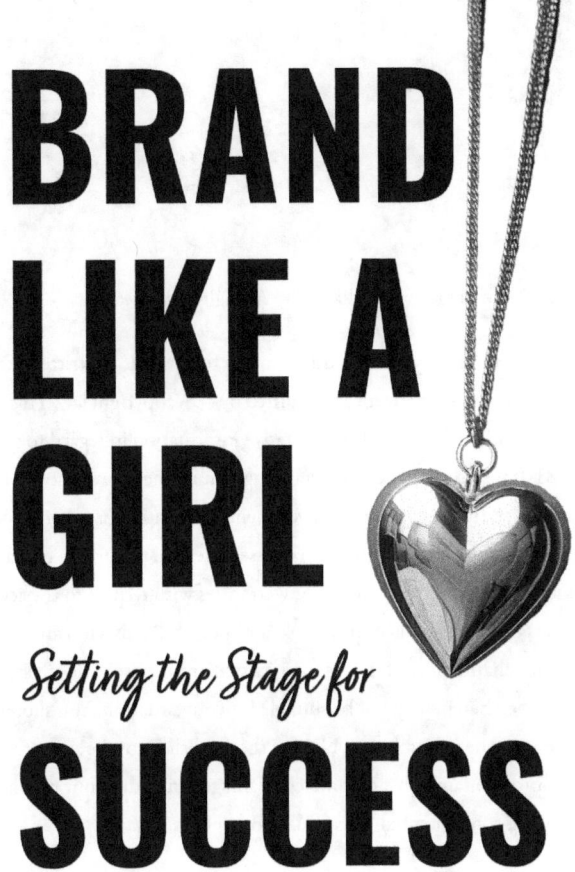

Setting the Stage for

SUCCESS

By Julie M. Adams, MSDM

Big Hook Media Inc™ Vancouver, Washington USA

BIG HOOK MEDIA

First Published 2024 by Big Hook Media Inc™

www.BigHookMedia.com 1st Edition, 2024

Library of Congress Control Number 2024926750

ISBN 979-8-9864177-0-7

Big Hook Media™ is more than a publisher; we're a community of storytellers, readers, creators, and dreamers. Join us as we continue to share stories that inspire minds and touch hearts.

Contents

Dedication

To every woman who has dared to dream, to lead, and to challenge the status quo—this is for you. May you find the strength to stand tall in your authenticity, the courage to amplify your voice, and the conviction to turn your vision into reality. To the allies and advocates who walk alongside us, thank you for fostering change and supporting the path to equality.

Together, we are rewriting the narrative to build a future where everyone can thrive.

Preface

Welcome to *Brand Like A Girl*, a manifesto for anyone
ready to redefine the landscape of branding and business
through a female-forward lens. At its core, this book is an
exploration of the untapped power that lies within strategies
that prioritize authenticity, inclusivity, and innovation—values
that are increasingly becoming non-negotiable in today's dynamic
business environment.

My journey into the heart of what it means to Brand Like A Girl
began not in boardrooms or business schools but in moments of
quiet rebellion against the prevailing currents of the advertising
world. During my early career, I found myself embedded in
an industry that, while creative, often clung to traditional,
conservative methods and overlooked the rich, diverse experiences
of women. It was amidst this backdrop that I challenged the
norms. I remember vividly a pivotal meeting where, fueled by a
mix of audacity and passion, I pitched a campaign rooted deeply in
my own experiences and observations as a woman. The campaign's
focus on authenticity and inclusivity struck a chord, marking
not just a professional triumph but a personal revelation: my

perspective as a woman was not merely a facet of my identity but a potent catalyst for creating brands that resonate deeply and authentically with audiences.

I wrote *Brand Like A Girl* for businesswomen, entrepreneurs, branding professionals, and anyone who sees the future of branding as deeply connected to empathy, strength, and resilience. This book draws on the unique challenges and opportunities that women face in business and branding, offering not just insights but practical, actionable strategies to harness your potential and create brands that endure and inspire.

The following pages will take you on a comprehensive journey—from understanding the current landscape of female-forward branding, through the mechanics of building and nurturing a brand with authenticity at its heart, to sustaining growth and impact in a constantly developing market. Each chapter equips you with the knowledge, tools, and confidence to carve out your own space in the branding world.

This preface would be incomplete without expressing my profound gratitude to the mentors who have guided, challenged, and inspired me. Their wisdom and support have been lighthouses on my voyage, illuminating paths less traveled and encouraging me to venture further.

To you, the reader, I invite you to join this exploration of new perspectives in branding and business. Whether you're in the early stages of dreaming up a brand or looking to infuse an established brand with renewed vitality and purpose, *Brand Like A Girl* is a testament to the power of viewing the world not just as it is, but as it could be when we dare to brand boldly and authentically.

May you find within these pages the spark to ignite your own revolution, to Brand Like A Girl, and in doing so, shape a future where businesses and brands reflect the richness and diversity of human experience.

Here's to crafting our own futures ~ Julie

Acknowledgements

Writing *Brand Like A Girl* has been a profoundly humbling and enlightening expedition, unveiling the essence of authentic branding of a tapestry of personal and collective journeys. The completion of this book is not a solitary achievement but a testament to the collective wisdom, love, and perseverance of many incredible souls who have touched my life and work in immeasurable ways.

First and foremost, I extend my deepest gratitude to my fellow author, mentor, and husband—Mike. Your steadfast support and insight have been my compass throughout this endeavor, as with all of my projects. The road trips spent reviewing ideas, your professional feedback, and unyielding encouragement reignited my creative spirit during moments of doubt and darkness. Mike, your unwavering belief in my vision lit the path when shadows of impostor syndrome loomed large, grounding me in my purpose, as you always do. You have always been my knight.

To the courageous women entrepreneurs who shared their stories, your narratives of resilience, authenticity, and triumph form the heartbeat of this book. Your openness, trust, and vibrance have not only inspired me but also countless others who will find solace and strength in your experiences. Your journeys remind us of all the power of our voices and the impact of living our truths.

To my children, whose love, teachings, and patience shaped not just the person I am today but the narratives within these pages. To my mom, thank you for always believing in me and encouraging me to chase my dreams—no matter how big.

To everyone who shared their time, wisdom, and encouragement, your influence permeates every page of this book. Your support and belief sustained the countless hours spent in solitude, wrestling with ideas and rewriting narratives, in this project. The moments of inspiration from unexpected places and times, the profound conversations, and the quiet gestures of encouragement have culminated in a reality far surpassing my dreams.

This book is an homage to each of you and the unspoken stories of perseverance, love, and transformation. It represents a shared victory, a common hope, and a collective voice that resonates with the message that authenticity and passion are the essence of branding—and life. My heartfelt gratitude and profound appreciation to everyone who embarked on this remarkable journey with me. Together, we've created something truly magical with *Brand Like A Girl*.

Introduction

Empowering Women to Lead the Branding Revolution

In an era where brands and their stories resonate louder than ever before, a revolution lies at the heart of the branding world—a movement propelled by authenticity, empathy, and innovation. *Brand Like A Girl* is not just a book; it's a call to arms for women ready to make their mark in the dynamic realm of branding and marketing. Here, we chart a course for redefining the branding landscape through an equitable lens, turning traditional strategies on their head and paving the way for a future where women's voices lead the narrative.

My journey in the branding industry, spanning over 15 years, has been rich with challenges, successes, and insights. Through my experience as a woman navigating the traditionally male-dominated fields of branding and marketing, I've garnered unique perspectives that have fueled my desire to drive innovation and change. Recognitions and accolades for my work uplifting women in business and pioneering brand innovation have only steeled my resolve. This book is a culmination of lessons learned, victories celebrated, and the universal truth that when women empower each other, incredible growth follows.

The representation of women in leadership roles within branding and marketing sectors is not just lacking—it's an opportunity missed for businesses to connect deeply with an audience that demands authenticity and empathy. *Brand Like A Girl* endeavors to fill this gap, providing a strategic blueprint for women by women. Through enriching case studies of successful women-led brands, this book sheds light on the strategies that make them stand out, championing the importance of leading with authenticity and a deep understanding of one's audience.

This book guides, inspires, and equips you, the reader, with the tools you need to excel. From dissecting the key elements that define successful women-led branding efforts to offering practical advice on how to implement these strategies, *Brand Like A Girl* serves as an essential handbook for anyone looking to make a significant impact in today's fast-evolving business landscape.

Rise above the noise. Brand Like A Girl, and let your authenticity be the beacon that guides others. Together, we will redefine the narrative, create meaningful connections, and establish brands that stand the test of time—all while navigating the business world with grace, strength, and indomitable spirit.

1
A Philosophy of Empowerment

Our journey begins by exploring the concept of 'Branding Like A Girl.' We'll dive into inspiring stories of women who have broken barriers, set new standards, and paved the way for change in the business world. Through case studies, insights, and practical tips, this guide will show you how to embrace inclusive branding principles shaped by women's unique experiences and leadership.

This is more than just a branding guide—it's a call to action. It urges businesses to embrace diversity, tell meaningful stories, and build brands that truly connect with people on an emotional level. Together, we can reshape the future of branding by amplifying women's voices and celebrating their impact on business and beyond.

Defining 'Branding Like A Girl'

Branding isn't just about logos and fonts—it's about building real, meaningful connections. To create brands that truly resonate, authenticity, empathy, and inclusivity are essential. That's the core of the 'Branding Like A Girl' philosophy. It's more than just a branding method; it's a movement that fosters genuine connections across diverse communities.

In this section, I'll outline the key principles of 'Branding Like A Girl.' These values are essential for building brands that are not only successful but also meaningful and impactful. By focusing on understanding, respect, and inclusivity, we can reshape branding strategies to leave a lasting, positive impact on both the market and society. Inclusivity becomes a driving force for growth and innovation, rather than an afterthought.

The result? Brands—whether for businesses or personal identity—that stand out for all the right reasons: authenticity, meaning, and purpose. Let's create something that truly makes a difference.

The Power of Authenticity

In today's digital world, where social media often mixes truth with fabrication, building customer trust means focusing on being real. Let's explore what authenticity means and how staying true to our values can shape our brand. By being authentic, we can create a relatable image that connects with people and stands out in a busy market. This book will share simple practices to stay authentic and show you how it helps build strong, lasting relationships with customers.

The Role of Empathy

Empathy, defined as "the capacity to comprehend and share the feelings of another person," stands as a formidable instrument in forging profound and enduring connections with customers and stakeholders. This unique ability enables individuals and organizations to see the world through others' eyes, fostering a deeper understanding and connection. In the upcoming section, we will study in depth the nuances of how nurturing empathy within teams and leadership can amplify branding efforts, elevating association with our audience. We will explore the ripple effect of empathy on creating a more substantial social impact, demonstrating how empathetic business practices can transform communities and industries at large. Through real-world examples and strategic insights, this discussion illuminates the path toward more empathetic and impactful branding for all of us.

Embracing Inclusivity

Inclusivity is the cornerstone of the initiative 'Branding Like A Girl,' which strongly advocates for diversity and representation in every aspect of branding. This book explores the concept that embracing an inclusive strategy not only cultivates a more authentic and relatable brand narrative, but also notably amplifies their reach and impact. By championing inclusivity, we can forge deeper connections with a more varied audience, guaranteeing that every individual feels recognized and valued in the multifaceted market of today.

Creating an inclusive brand isn't about checking boxes or ticking off a list—it's about genuinely embracing diverse voices and perspectives in every part of our strategy and communication. When we take this approach, it not only makes our message richer but also reflects the real-world diversity of our audience. And let's be honest, in a time when people are craving authenticity and meaningful connections, inclusivity is a game-changer. It helps brands shine and creates an unforgettable impression.

The Significance of Storytelling in Branding

Woven through this book is an exploration of the intricate role stories play as a fundamental element in building strong, resonant brands. Together, we'll examine how these narratives have the unique ability to motivate audiences, impart valuable lessons, and, most critically, empower consumers and communities to connect with us on a deeper level. Stories surpass mere telling; we experience them on a subconscious level, engaging the listener's empathy and imagination. This emotional response is what grants stories their immense influence and lasting impact, enabling us to forge deep, meaningful connections with our audience. Such stories articulate our values, aspirations, and the essence of our identity, shaping how consumers perceive us.

Exploring 'Branding Like A Girl' Through Real-World Examples

In the introductory section of *Brand Like A Girl*, I laid the groundwork for revolutionizing branding as we know it. I introduced a novel paradigm—one that champions the power of authenticity, the significance of empathy, and the necessity of inclusivity. This foundation is not just theoretical; it represents a transformative shift in how we can best connect with our audience in a way that promotes substantial customer loyalty.

Real-Life Brand Success Stories

The Wing: Revolutionizing Co-Working with Community and Empathy

The inception of The Wing represented a groundbreaking venture into the co-working space sector, but with a distinctive twist that set it apart: it explicitly catered to female professionals. This was not merely a place to work; it was a space designed to foster a sense of community among its members. By focusing on empathetic design and inclusive programming, The Wing meticulously crafted an environment conducive to both professional growth and personal development for women.

The brand carefully constructed its narrative around themes of empowerment and solidarity. This approach did not just speak to its audience—it resonated with them, creating a profound sense of belonging. Members of The Wing felt seen, heard, and supported in a way that was rare in traditional co-working spaces. This strong resonance led to the formation of a loyal community, a testament to the brand's success in understanding and meeting the needs of its members.

The Wing's success story provides the significance of empathetic engagement and the creation of spaces that prioritize inclusivity. It speaks to how modern businesses can thrive by not just offering services, but by cultivating environments that resonate with and enrich the lives of their community members. The Wing's innovative model demonstrates the untapped potential in the business landscape for spaces that are not only about work but also about building meaningful connections and supporting individual journeys.

Glossier: Beauty Redefined through Authentic Customer Dialogues

Glossier, a brand that has revolutionized the beauty industry, initially debuted as a modest blog before blossoming into a formidable entity that has drastically altered the traditional, hierarchical beauty narrative. By meticulously paying attention to the desires and needs of its engaged community, Glossier has forged a new, innovative path in how it connects with consumers, offering an interaction that is both authentic and groundbreaking. Its commitment to actively listening to its consumers has completely inverted the conventional model of product development. Glossier's distinctive approach entails gathering feedback and analytics from its audience through a meticulous analysis of comments, reviews and social media interactions. This critical information significantly influences both the creation and continuous refinement of Glossier's product line.

In stark contrast to traditional marketing angles, which typically rely on a highly polished, idealized concept of beauty to drive product sales, Glossier has courageously opted for an alternative route. It celebrates real, unfiltered beauty by featuring multicultural, unretouched models in its advertising campaigns. The deliberate choice to present diverse natural beauty connected strongly with audiences weary of the beauty industry's unrealistic ideals. This genuine, inclusive approach has distinguished Glossier in the competitive beauty market, cultivating a profound sense of trust and loyalty among its consumer base. This has nurtured a passionate community of followers who feel genuinely seen and heard.

The meteoric rise of Glossier is not merely a marketing success story but emblematically represents a seismic paradigm shift within the beauty industry. It exemplifies that authenticity, inclusivity, and a heartfelt commitment to listening to and valuing the voices of consumers can wield a remarkable influence on a brand's trajectory. Through its pioneering initiatives, Glossier has not only solidified its presence in the market, but has also ignited a crucial dialogue about the future of beauty branding. The brand's capacity to engage with individuals on a deeply personal level, its celebration of authentic beauty, and its efforts to build a community rooted in shared values and ideals have elevated it from a simple blog to a breath of fresh air within the beauty sphere.

As Glossier continues to evolve and broaden its product range, it loyally adheres to its mission of challenging and redefining conventional beauty norms. This persistent pursuit demonstrates that a brand can achieve both commercial success and contribute positively to societal discourse, proving that Glossier is indeed a trailblazer, setting new standards for what it means to be a socially conscious beauty brand in today's world.

REI's #OptOutside Campaign: Aligning Brand Values with Conscious Consumerism

REI, the renowned outdoor retail cooperative, made a groundbreaking decision to counteract the consumerism frenzy typically associated with Black Friday. They launched the #OptOutside campaign, a revolutionary initiative encouraging individuals and families to forego the shopping madness and instead spend their time enjoying the great outdoors—*clever*.

REI's decision was based on its core values of environmental care and fostering adventure. It wasn't just an effective marketing strategy, but a reflection of the company's commitment to environmental conservation and the well-being of its community.

The campaign struck a chord with environmentally conscious consumers and those yearning for authentic experiences over material possessions. It didn't just encourage people to rethink their Black Friday habits; it ignited a broader movement towards appreciating nature and prioritizing personal well-being. By aligning its brand story with the societal shift towards sustainable living and a growing consumer desire for meaningful experiences, REI not only strengthened its community but also significantly boosted brand loyalty.

The #OptOutside campaign has been a catalyst for change within the retail industry, prompting other brands to reevaluate their Black Friday campaigns. REI's initiative has shown that it's possible for a company to stay true to its values while still achieving success, proving that ethical business practices and a strong, value-driven brand narrative can lead to deeper customer relationships and a loyal consumer base.

Navigating Intersectionality and Societal Change

'Branding Like A Girl' not only intersects with but also champions movements such as conscious consumerism and the evolving role of women in the business landscape. This reflects a growing demand among consumers for brands that not only talk the talk but *walk the walk* with ethical practices, embracing diversity, and forging genuine connections with their audience.

The democratization of technology has played a pivotal role in amplifying these diverse voices, particularly with female leadership and its impact on society. This spotlight on women in power positions has further accelerated a shift towards more human-centric branding, where empathy, authenticity, and social responsibility take center stage. Brands that not only recognize but also firmly adapt to these interwoven dynamics are set to shape the future for success in the marketplace and stand to drive profound, meaningful societal change. In doing so, they contribute to a more inclusive and equitable business environment, showcasing how the principles of 'Branding Like A Girl' can lead to a broader transformation across all industries.

Practical Steps Towards Female-Driven Branding

For entrepreneurs looking to infuse the bold principles of 'Branding Like A Girl' into their brand, the journey starts with a series of strategic, impactful steps. It's all about *truly* understanding your audience—not just on the surface, but digging deep into their needs, values, and preferences. Inclusivity isn't just a trendy term here. It's a genuine commitment to reflecting diverse voices and experiences in your brand's story. And let's not forget authenticity. Every ad, message, and product should stay true to your brand's identity while creating a meaningful connection with your audience. Ready to make your brand unforgettable? *It starts here.*

Creating a brand that vibrates with the frequency of personal connection involves more than just clever marketing tactics; it requires a commitment to align every marketing effort and product development with the core values of empathy, empowerment, and innovation. This implies a relentless dedication to understanding and anticipating the needs of the consumer, fostering a brand environment that champions empowerment in all its forms, and continuously pushing the boundaries of innovation to meet and exceed customer expectations. At its core, 'Branding Like A Girl' is about infusing these principles into every part of your brand's identity. This helps it stand out in a crowded market and leave a meaningful, lasting impact. It's about uplifting, inspiring, and connecting with your audience on a deeper level. These five steps are your roadmap to get started—let the journey begin!

1. **Authenticity Audit**: Initiate a thorough assessment to gauge the alignment of your brand with its inherent identity and foundational values. The importance of authenticity cannot be overstated—it resonates on a profound level with audiences, fostering a sense of trust and reliability that is indispensable for

cultivating long-lasting customer relationships. This extensive process entails a detailed examination of your brand's overall messaging, operational efforts, and every touchpoint of customer interaction. It's about ensuring that every facet of your brand consistently reflects its true essence, from the way you communicate on social media to the customer service experience you provide. Diving deep into these areas can uncover knowledge that helps reinforce your brand's authenticity, making it more appealing and relevant to your target audience.

2. **Empathetic Engagement**: To truly elevate the customer experience, implement messaging that goes beyond surface-level interactions by deeply understanding and effectively addressing your audience's needs and concerns. This involves emphasizing active listening, where you fully concentrate, understand, respond, and then remember what is being said. Providing heartfelt, thoughtful responses is crucial to ensuring that every transaction is transformed into a meaningful interaction. By doing so, you not only foster stronger connections with your customers, but also build trust and loyalty. This methodical approach to empathy and engagement helps in transforming customers into passionate advocates who are more likely to return and recommend your services to others. Cultivating such an environment where every customer feels valued and understood

can significantly enhance the overall customer journey, leading to sustained business growth and a strong, positive brand reputation.

3. **Inclusivity in Action**: In today's global market, it's more important than ever for brands to embody inclusivity by actively reflecting a broad range of perspectives and stories within their messaging, marketing strategy, and product lines. This approach is not just about ensuring every customer feels seen and valued; it's about acknowledging the deep values of different human experiences and leveraging that diversity to create more resonant and impactful offerings. Embracing such diversity goes beyond merely fulfilling a moral imperative or checking a box for corporate social responsibility. It acts as a powerful catalyst for innovation, growth, and competitive advantage. By intentionally integrating a wide array of viewpoints, backgrounds, and experiences into their operations and output, companies can foster a more creative, inclusive, and dynamic environment. This stimulates innovation by challenging conventional thinking and encouraging new ideas that lead to the development of better solutions, products, and services. By establishing a stronger connection with a broader and more varied audience, businesses can enhance customer loyalty, expand their market reach, and drive forward with greater momentum in an increasingly interconnected

world. The commitment to inclusivity is not only a
testament to a brand's values, but a strategic asset that
propels the organization toward a more prosperous and
equitable future.

4. **Collaborative Storytelling**: Engage your audience by
sharing compelling narratives that reflect the core values
and ethos of your brand. These stories should not only
embody the spirit of your brand, but also resonate with
your audience on a deeply personal level, creating a
powerful emotional bond. The power of storytelling lies
in its ability to bring people together, sparking inspiration
and motivating collective action towards a shared vision
or goal. This is because stories have the unique ability
to transport people to different worlds, allowing them
to experience new perspectives and emotions, thereby
fostering a strong sense of community and belonging.
By weaving together tales that are both authentic and
relatable, you create an emotional connection that can
significantly enhance the impact of your message. This
approach not only increases engagement but also builds
trust and loyalty among your audience, making your
brand more memorable and influential.

5. **Strategic Partnerships**: To significantly amplify your
message and enhance your brand's visibility in the
market, consider entering into collaborations with brands

or influencers that resonate with your core principles and objectives. This strategic move is not just about expanding your reach; it's about tapping into new audiences by aligning with partners who share your values and vision for success. Pursuing these strategic partnerships allows you to leverage diverse platforms and networks, thereby magnifying your impact through the foundation of shared values and mutual goals. Such collaborations are not merely transactional; they are transformative, enabling both parties to benefit from the enhanced credibility and heightened interest that comes from being associated with each other. This approach creates a synergistic effect, propelling all parties involved towards greater success and visibility in their respective domains. The key to unlocking these benefits lies in carefully selecting partners whose vision, audience, and business goals align with yours, thereby ensuring that every collaboration is powerful and purpose-driven.

By forging such powerful alliances, you can drive meaningful engagement and attract a broader audience, fostering long-term growth. This strategy not only enhances your brand's credibility in the eyes of your current and potential customers, but also sets the stage for a collaborative ecosystem where *everyone involved thrives*. Strategic partnerships are the key to building a bold, resilient brand that thrives in today's competitive market. They create immediate impact while fueling long-term growth, helping your business stand out and succeed.

As we chart the path forward together, 'Branding Like A Girl' holds the promise of transforming not just businesses, but industries at large. By championing authenticity, empathy, inclusivity, and the power of collective storytelling, women can create deeper connections. We can drive positive change and achieve unprecedented success. The case studies of The Wing, Glossier, and REI, along with outlined insights later in this book, serve as perfect examples of what's possible when businesses dare to *Brand Like A Girl*.

The evolution of this movement reveals an exciting frontier for women ready to engage with their audiences authentically and meaningfully. The intersection of branding with socio-cultural movements pinpoints the importance of building brands that not only speak to consumers on a personal level, but also reflect broader societal values and aspirations. The future belongs to those who lead with heart, courage, and authenticity. Female-driven branding isn't just a passing trend—it's a powerful force shaping business success and creating a meaningful impact in the world.

Let's keep pushing boundaries, breaking stereotypes, and boldly Brand Like A Girl!

#BrandingLikeAGirl #FemaleLeadership #Authenticity #Empathy #Inclusivity

Inspirational Stories of Women Who Have 'Branded Like A Girl'

Now let's examine the inspiring journeys of renowned female entrepreneurs who have carved their niches and built successful businesses with innovative and unique methods of branding. From fashion to technology, these trailblazing women are breaking barriers and reshaping industries. Their incredible achievements inspire a new generation of entrepreneurs to dream bigger and aim higher. Their stories of dedication, creativity, and bold leadership reveal how they turned challenges into stepping stones on their journey to success.

The remarkable journeys of iconic female leaders such as Oprah Winfrey, Sheryl Sandberg, and Indra Nooyi offer rich, valuable lessons on personal branding, resilience, and breaking through barriers. These women have not only carved out spaces for themselves in their respective fields but have also paved the way for future generations of women to follow. Let's examine the strategies they employed to overcome challenges and the wisdom they have imparted on leadership, empowerment, and success. Through their powerful case studies, I'll reveal how they've transformed the business world for women, sparking inspiration and offering a roadmap for anyone ready to make their mark.

Oprah Winfrey: A Beacon of Leadership, Empowerment, and Success

Oprah Winfrey, a name synonymous with resilience, empowerment, and groundbreaking success, is a luminary whose life and career offer invaluable lessons in leadership and perseverance. This case study explores the values that Oprah employed to overcome challenges, her profound impact on the business landscape, particularly for women, and the enduring wisdom she has imparted along the way.

Overcoming Challenges through Authenticity and Empathy

At the heart of Oprah's unprecedented success was her groundbreaking approach to talk show hosting. By focusing on authentic conversations, empathy, and connecting with her audience on a personal level, Oprah revolutionized daytime television. This strategy not only differentiated 'The Oprah Winfrey Show' but also set a new standard for broadcasts worldwide. Her heartfelt curiosity about people's stories and her gift for creating a safe, welcoming space for honest, vulnerable conversations made her beloved by millions.

Cultivating Literacy and Influence through Oprah's Book Club

Oprah's Book Club redefined public engagement with literature, showcasing her role as a tastemaker and her commitment to education. By spotlighting a mix of novels, many of which were by unknown authors, Oprah elevated readership and significantly impacted book sales, illustrating the power of her endorsement. This initiative underlines Oprah's belief in the transformative power of education and literacy as tools for empowerment.

Perseverance in the Face of Adversity

Oprah's career trajectory is well-punctuated with challenges, from early career setbacks to public criticism. However, she navigated these obstacles with an unwavering spirit of resilience, using each experience as a stepping stone for personal growth. Her openness about these struggles signifies hope and encouragement for others facing similar hurdles, embodying the essence of persevering in the face of adversity.

Entrepreneurship and Vision—The Establishment of Harpo Productions and OWN

Oprah's establishment of Harpo Productions and the subsequent launch of the Oprah Winfrey Network highlight her entrepreneurial spirit and vision to create media that empowers and inspires. Through these ventures, Oprah has created platforms for diverse voices and stories, particularly those of women and minorities, empowering a new generation of content creators and media professionals.

Oprah's Enduring Wisdom

"Think like a queen. A queen is not afraid to fail. Failing is a another stepping stone to greatness."

—Oprah Winfrey

This quote from Oprah encapsulates the essence of her approach to life and business. It speaks to the importance of self-confidence, the courage to face failure, and the resilience to continue striving for success.

Business Impact and Cultural Shift

Oprah's influence extends beyond personal empowerment, significantly shaping the business landscape. Her approach to talk show hosting has forced a cultural reevaluation of content, making the media landscape more inclusive and relatable. Her ventures demonstrate the economic and societal value of diverse storytelling, providing inspiration and pathways for women in entrepreneurship and media.

Key Takeaways and Concluding Thoughts

Oprah's career offers profound lessons in creating space for oneself while paving the way for future generations. Her emphasis on authenticity, empathetic engagement, and the strategic creation of platforms for empowerment have not only defined her legacy, but have also transformed the business landscape for women. Oprah's success emphasizes the importance of self-belief, resilience, and the pursuit of one's passions against all odds.

Her life and career offer invaluable examples for those looking to make their mark on the world, broadening the significance of leadership, empowerment, and the capacity to inspire change. Through her example, Oprah continues to elevate the dialogue around success, leadership, and the potential within us all to overcome our challenges and achieve greatness.

***

Sheryl Sandberg Case Study: Pioneering Leadership and Advocacy for Gender Equality in the Business World

Sheryl Sandberg is a name synonymous with transformative leadership and unwavering commitment to gender equality in the workplace. Her illustrious career spanning technology, business strategy, and advocacy provides a compelling narrative on leadership, the power of voice in advocating for women's rights, and strategic decision-making. This case study explores Sandberg's multifaceted career, focusing on her leadership style, advocacy for gender equality through the 'Lean In' initiative, strategic contributions to Facebook, and her approach to work-life balance and career navigation.

Leadership Style

Empowerment, collaboration, and resilience characterize Sheryl Sandberg's leadership approach. Sheryl, through her role as Chief Operating Officer at Facebook, showcased an exemplary model of leadership that emphasized the importance of giving voice to the voiceless and fostering an environment of mutual respect and support. Her resilience in the face of personal and professional challenges has served as an inspiration for leaders around the globe. Sandberg's leadership is not just about directing from the top; it's about nurturing talent, encouraging constructive feedback, and leveraging team strengths to achieve common goals.

Real-World Example

At Facebook, Sandberg championed open communication and mentorship programs that empowered employees at all levels to speak up and contribute their best work. Her initiative to establish Lean-In Circles within the community facilitated a culture of support and empowerment, extending well beyond the walls of Facebook.

Gender Equality Advocacy

The launch of the 'Lean In' initiative marked a pivotal moment in the global discourse on gender equality in the workplace. Sandberg's personal dedication to addressing the challenges faced by women in corporate environments spurred a movement that encouraged women to aspire to leadership positions and challenge societal norms.

Business Impact and Cultural Shift

'Lean In' resonated with millions, igniting conversations about gender roles, biases, and the systemic barriers that hinder women's career advancement. Sandberg's work has not only raised awareness, but also inspired actionable changes in policies and practices within organizations worldwide.

Business Strategy at Facebook

Sheryl Sandberg's strategic acumen was instrumental in scaling Facebook from a popular social network to a global powerhouse with substantial cultural influence. Her focus on monetization, advertising models, and international expansion played a significant role in Facebook's growth trajectory.

Strategic Decisions

One of Sandberg's key strategies was the development of targeted advertising solutions that leveraged Facebook's extensive user data, transforming the platform into an invaluable tool for businesses and advertisers. This move not only propelled Facebook's revenue but also redefined social media marketing into what we know today.

Work-Life Balance and Career Navigation

Balancing a high-profile career and personal life isn't easy, but Sandberg has managed to do it with grace and resilience. She's shared some important lessons along the way that professionals everywhere can learn from. Her push for workplace flexibility, parental leave, and better support systems has really helped shape the conversation about juggling career goals and personal responsibilities. I really wish this had been around back when I was in the corporate world.

Key Takeaways and Concluding Thoughts

Sandberg's approach shows the importance of setting boundaries, prioritizing self-care, and seeking support networks, both professionally and personally. Her openness about her challenges for coping serves as a guiding light for others seeking to find equilibrium in their lives.

Sheryl Sandberg's legacy transcends her accomplishments at Facebook and her advocacy work. Her leadership style—a blend of empathy, resilience, and unwavering support for her teams—alongside her relentless pursuit of gender equality, sets her apart as a trailblazer in the business world. Through strategic foresight, she has significantly impacted Facebook's ascendancy in the digital era, while her 'Lean In' initiative continues to empower women worldwide to achieve their fullest potential. Sandberg's narrative is a powerful testament to the influence of visionary leadership and the enduring impact of advocating for change, offering profound perspectives for gender equality advocates, women in business, and entrepreneurs alike.

***

Indra Nooyi: A Legacy of Transformative Leadership at PepsiCo

Hailing from Chennai, India, Indra Nooyi charted an illustrious path that led her to become one of the most influential leaders in the global business arena. With a keen intellect and a determination to break through the glass ceiling, Nooyi's leadership tenure at PepsiCo has been marked by groundbreaking achievements and a visionary approach to corporate leadership.

Her Tenure as CEO of PepsiCo

Indra Nooyi assumed the role of CEO at PepsiCo in 2006, a time when the company was facing immense competition and shifting consumer preferences. Under her stewardship, PepsiCo not only navigated these challenges but also emerged stronger, more resilient, and poised for sustainable growth. Her Key

Achievement? Financial growth and doubling net profits. Nooyi's strategic foresight and ability to drive financial performance was the driving force for PepsiCo's successes that year.

Focus on Healthier Products and Growth in Health & Wellness Category

Recognizing the shifting consumer demand towards healthier options, Nooyi led the company's pivot towards products that not only satisfied appetites but also contributed to well-being, cementing PepsiCo's presence in the health and wellness sector.

'Performance with Purpose' Initiative and Corporate Social Responsibility

Nooyi's 'Performance with Purpose' initiative emphasized her belief in the power of corporations to effect positive change. Under this initiative, PepsiCo committed to sustainability and social responsibility, significantly enhancing the company's public image.

Recognition and High-Profile Acquisitions

Nooyi's visionary leadership garnered her the #2 spot on Fortune Magazine's list of Most Powerful Women in Business in 2015. Meanwhile, her strategic oversight of acquisitions, like Tropicana and Quaker Oats, played a crucial role in diversifying PepsiCo's portfolio.

Visionary Leadership

Nooyi's forward-thinking approach was instrumental in steering PepsiCo towards long-term growth and sustainability.

Strategic Decision-Making

Her ability to make bold, strategic decisions enabled the company to capitalize on new opportunities and remain competitive in a rapidly changing industry.

Commitment to Innovation and Adaptability

Nooyi fostered a culture of innovation at PepsiCo, allowing the company to adapt to changing consumer preferences and stay ahead of trends.

Effective Communication and Team Empowerment

Through effective communication and a commitment to inclusivity, Nooyi empowered her teams to achieve their best, enhancing collaboration and innovation across the company.

Resilience and Determination

Facing the corporate world's challenges head-on, Nooyi's resilience and determination set a powerful example for women in leadership.

Financial and Market Performance

PepsiCo's robust financial and market performance under Nooyi's leadership reflected the successful execution of strategic initiatives and a deep understanding of global market dynamics.

Company Culture and Employee Engagement

Nooyi's leadership positively impacted PepsiCo's company culture, fostering a sense of belonging and encouraging employee engagement and innovation.

Public Image and Brand Perception

Under Nooyi's guidance, PepsiCo strengthened its public image, emerging as a leader in corporate social responsibility and ethical business practices.

Key Takeaways and Concluding Thoughts

Navigating the competitive landscape and implementing wide scale changes were significant challenges that Nooyi adeptly managed. Her tenure stressed the importance of balancing shareholder interests with social responsibility, offering valuable lessons in leadership.

Indra Nooyi's transformative leadership at PepsiCo stands as an inspiring case study not only for women in business, but for all aspiring leaders. Her strategic vision, commitment to innovation, and deep sense of corporate social responsibility have not only reshaped PepsiCo's trajectory but also set new standards for the global business community. Nooyi's focus on long-term growth, resilience in the face of challenges, and dedication to empowering her teams signifies the critical role of inclusive and forward-thinking leadership in driving success. As the corporate world continues to evolve, Nooyi's legacy fosters innovation and the achievement of sustainable growth.

The Evolution of Authenticity and Inclusion in Branding

In the landscape of modern entrepreneurship, the stories and strategies of female entrepreneurs have emerged as symbols of innovation and resilience. Iconic women like Coco Chanel and Maya Angelou, with their incredible contributions to the world, have inspired everyday women to step up and 'Brand Like A Girl.'

Shifting from earlier case studies to the impact of iconic female leaders and entrepreneurs, these stories showcase success built on authenticity, empathy, inclusiveness, and smart branding. From breaking into traditionally male-dominated industries to rethink business approaches with fresh, innovative ideas, these women have shown incredible resilience and vision. Their achievements don't just inspire future generations—they're actively shaping the future of business by creating spaces that value diversity, creativity, and meaningful connections.

Pioneering Fashion with Inclusivity

Sarah's big moment wasn't just a win for her growing brand—it was a huge step forward in pushing back against the fashion industry's narrow standards. "Hello! How can I help you today?" The customer service representative greeted Sarah with a friendly smile emoji. Excitement bubbled in her stomach as she typed in her latest order for her fashion line, which had just been featured in a major magazine.

Sarah had always been passionate about fashion and design, but she noticed a huge gap in the market when it came to inclusivity. As a plus-size woman herself, she struggled to find stylish clothing that fit her body type. She knew there were many other women out there facing the same issue. So, Sarah decided to take matters into her own hands and launch her own fashion line focused on inclusive sizing and representation of all body types. It was not an easy journey, as she faced skepticism from investors and industry gatekeepers, but her pop-up event was a massive success, and it wasn't just about celebrating her achievements. It highlighted a bigger cultural shift toward inclusivity and diversity, pushing the fashion industry to redefine its approach to beauty, customer engagement, and representation.

Sarah's story is a powerful testament to the undeniable power of determination and direct action in the face of widespread skepticism and entrenched norms. Her journey serves not not only as a source of inspiration but also as a model for others aspiring to be entrepreneurs and innovators. Sarah's story is a powerful reminder of how one person, armed with a bold vision and unshakable determination, can challenge and transform the status quo. Her actions have sparked a revolution in the fashion industry, opening the door to a future that's more inclusive and diverse. With passion and perseverance, she's proven that real, lasting change is possible—and her journey inspires others to do the same.

Redefining Tech Engagement

Alex's courageous decision to confront criticism head-on, rather than shying away from it, transformed a potentially devastating crisis into a pivotal growth opportunity for her consulting company.

Alex: "I know many of you are worried about the changes happening right now. It's completely valid to feel uncertain."

Staff member: "But how do we know these changes will actually benefit us?"

Alex: "That's a fair question. Let me break it down for you. We've carefully analyzed the situation and ensured these updates address the primary concerns raised. Your feedback was crucial in shaping this."

Staff member: "What if things still don't work out?"

Alex: "I understand that fear. We're committed to ongoing support and adjustments as needed. This isn't a onetime fix—it's a continuous process, and your input will always be a part of it."

By choosing to engage directly with her audience's concerns, showing a genuine openness and a firm commitment to diversity and inclusivity, she did much more than just salvage the company's image. She effectively set a new standard for transparent and accountable communication within the tech industry, an area where many companies struggle to find their footing. This proactive approach diffused the immediate situation and contributed to building a deeper, more trusting relationship with her client. This case is a great example of how to handle technology storms, showing how challenges can be reframed into opportunities to grow your brand and take the lead in corporate responsibility.

Sustainable Practices as Brand Cornerstones

Maria's heartfelt social media post didn't just save her struggling business—it showed how much people value honesty and genuine commitment to the environment.

> At GreenPath, we believe actions speak louder than words. That's why we're proud to share that 100% of our packaging is now biodegradable, and we've partnered with local communities to plant over 10,000 trees this year! Your support helps us make a real impact, and we're committed to doing even more. Let's create a greener future together
> #Sustainability #EcoFriendly #RealChange

Her story is a glorious reminder that sustainability isn't just a bonus anymore—it's essential. Eco-friendly practices have become a defining factor that sets a brand apart. It's not just about doing the right thing; it's about connecting with people who care and showing you're different in a world where thoughtful choices really matter.

Diane's Fusion of Self and Brand

Diane's journey from a passionate sustainability advocate to a prominent ethical fashion designer serves as a compelling testament to the power of personal branding that is deeply intertwined with one's core values. Her remarkable evolution spearheads the significant impact of aligning personal ethos with her public persona, setting a new standard for what authenticity in action looks like. Diane's success story is not just inspiring but acts as a strategic blueprint for authenticity, demonstrating unequivocally how personal conviction and steadfast commitment to one's beliefs can serve as a powerful differentiator in a crowded and competitive market.

> *"Building a brand rooted in ethical fashion has been one of the most rewarding yet challenging journeys I've ever taken. There are days when I feel immense pride seeing customers who choose sustainability, but there are also moments of doubt—like how to balance fair wages with affordable pricing or finding suppliers who truly align with our values. It's not perfect, and I'm constantly learning, but I believe these challenges*

are worth facing to create significant change in the
industry."

—Diane

Through her carefully curated content and deliberate engagement mission, Diane has forged a strong connection with her community. Her approach of transparent storytelling, where she shares not only her triumphs but also the challenges she faces in the ethical fashion space, resonates deeply with her audience. Diane's efforts to foster partnerships with brands that share her values of sustainability and ethical production amplify her message and impact. This strategic collaboration extends her influence and reinforces the authenticity of her brand.

Diane's strategy for engaging with her community offers a wealth of practical tactics for brands aiming to deepen customer relationships and carve out a distinctive position in the marketplace. From transparent storytelling that builds trust and credibility to fostering partnerships based on shared values, which enhance brand alignment and loyalty, Diane exemplifies how individual influencers and brands alike can thrive by being true to their values and consistently communicating this truth to their audience. Her story pinpoints the importance of authenticity, conviction, and strategic community engagement in building a successful and influential personal brand.

Leveraging Historical and Cultural Insights

The enduring influence of female trailblazers such as Coco Chanel and Maya Angelou extends far beyond the confines of their respective fields of fashion and literature. These remarkable women have shaped the broader narrative around women's roles in society and business, breaking barriers and setting new standards for what women can achieve. Their legacies continue to inspire not only in their respective industries but also across the societal fabric, encouraging a more inclusive and equitable world in any industry.

Understanding the historical and cultural context of their achievements is crucial for modern entrepreneurs. It provides them with a richer palette for crafting brands that not only honor these legacies but also push the boundaries of creativity and inclusion. By following the stories of these pioneering women, entrepreneurs can glean a thorough understanding of resilience, innovation, and the power of challenging the status quo. This enhanced understanding can be seamlessly integrated into business practices and brand narratives that resonate with purpose and impact. By doing so, the pioneering legacy of women like Chanel and Angelou is honored and celebrated, inspiring today's female entrepreneurs to carry their trailblazing spirit forward.

Cultivating Empathy and Diversity

This movement towards inclusivity and diversity in branding isn't merely a nod to political correctness. Rather, it defines a profound recognition of the rich, varied experiences and knowledge that women contribute to every aspect of business and society. By actively integrating these perspectives into their branding efforts, companies can craft messaging that not only resonates more deeply with a broader audience but also fosters a more authentic and impactful connection with consumers. This approach enhances brand loyalty and perception while driving forward a more inclusive and just business environment.

The continuous evolution of female empowerment movements and diversity initiatives is reshaping the business landscape. These shifts unveil the importance of female leadership and its ability to foster innovation, drive empathy, and create inclusive spaces. Enterprises that recognize and harness these strengths are not only contributing to a more equitable world, but are also positioning themselves as leaders in the next wave of business evolution.

A Call to Action for 'Branding Like A Girl'

Our exploration of the dynamic interplay between femininity, branding, and leadership culminates in a compelling call to action. The stories and strategies I've shared not only celebrate the achievements of women in business but also challenge readers to reflect on how they can incorporate these concepts into their own brand-building efforts.

The future of business is calling for a bold shift—one that embraces heart, inclusivity, and empathy. With the 'Branding Like A Girl' philosophy, women are empowered to chart this new path using their unique perspectives and values to build brands that truly connect. It's more than a strategy; it's a movement to create brands that inspire and resonate on a deeper level.

Your Role in the Movement Is Our Path Forward

The narrative of female-driven branding is still being written, with each entrepreneur contributing to a diverse and vibrant assembly of success stories. The lessons gleaned from the journeys of these pioneering women are more than historical footnotes; they are signposts guiding us towards a future where brands built on authenticity, empathy, and inclusivity not only thrive but also redefine the essence of success.

As we turn the page on this chapter, I invite you to consider how you can embody the spirit of 'Branding Like A Girl' in your entrepreneurial endeavors. Branding isn't about logos or flashy marketing—it's about the stories we share, the communities we create, and the values we stand for. *That's where the actual power lies.* The world is eagerly awaiting the unique story *only you can tell*, your distinctive vision and your inspired leadership.

Now is the time to step up and brand with boldness, passion, and an unshakable belief in the transformative power of feminine perspectives. It's time to spark change and inspire others by celebrating the strength, the creativity, and the resilience of female leadership. Your voice matters—let's lead the charge together!

The Journey Ahead

As I bring this chapter to a close, I want to extend a heartfelt invitation—an earnest plea—for you to adopt these principles and to fully and fearlessly embody them in every aspect of your life. The rapidly evolving landscape of the modern business world is not just suggesting but emphatically demanding a new breed of leader. This leader is much more than an administrator or a manager; they are a visionary, a new type of storyteller, one who has the unique ability to weave compelling visions into tangible reality, inspiring unprecedented change and fostering innovation at every single turn.

Your Next Steps

This call to action is for those who are ready to boldly step into the unknown with unwavering conviction, to lead with unparalleled courage, and to rewrite the rules of engagement for the betterment of all. It is a call for those who see beyond the horizon, who are not afraid to challenge the status quo and who are ready to spearhead a movement towards a more inclusive, innovative, and sustainable future.

By embracing these principles, you will not only become a catalyst for change within your organization but also set a new standard of leadership that others will aspire to. This journey requires a commitment to continuous learning, an openness to adapt, and a willingness to embrace challenges as opportunities for growth. Are you ready to answer this call, to become the leader that the future business world needs? The core spirit of 'Branding Like A Girl' isn't something external; it resides deeply within you. It's woven into the fabric of your personal stories, the values you uphold, and the visions that propel you forward. Our future on the path we will walk together hinges on our collective courage to brand with boldness, to love with depth, and to lead with our hearts wide open, *unafraid of vulnerability.*

I genuinely hope you are ready to claim your rightful place in this unfolding narrative. Because embarking on this journey is more than the start of a new chapter in a book—it's the dawn of a powerful movement. A movement where each page turned is a step towards embracing our true selves, and every word read, a call to action. This is your invitation to join a community of trailblazers, to become a proponent of change and to inspire those around you.

So, I ask you once more—are you ready? Ready to join something greater than yourself, to play a meaningful role in a story far bigger than any of us? This is much more than just a book—it's the beginning of our collective revolution.

2

Breaking Barriers

In today's progressive world, a startling statistic serves as a wake-up call, underscoring the persistent barriers that women in business continue to face. Despite significant advancements, the path to leadership is often fraught with obstacles that are invisible to others yet immense for those who encounter them. This chapter is dedicated to unraveling the complexities of these challenges, sharing strategies for overcoming them, and celebrating the stories of women who have blazed trails in the business realm.

The Reality of Barriers: Leadership Narratives of Resilience and Innovation

We begin by examining both historical and current obstacles that women encounter in the business world. From systemic biases embedded within corporate structures to the subtler forms of resistance met in everyday interactions, these barriers are multifaceted. Yet, the resilience and ingenuity displayed by women in navigating this landscape are nothing short of inspirational.

Now we will discover modern experiences that detail the systemic biases and challenges women face in business. From being overlooked for promotions to facing micro-aggressions, these anecdotes serve as powerful reminders that barriers still exist and require solutions.

Empowering Encounter: Breaking Biases with Confidence and Insight

In the middle of a busy corporate world, an important meeting was about to kick off in a bright, neatly arranged conference room. The polished wooden table and comfy chairs were set up in a semi-circle, and a big high-definition screen promised some exciting ideas ahead. The room had that professional vibe, mixed with a bit of formality, and you could feel the buzz of anticipation as everyone got ready for some intense discussions. Among all the participants, one person stood out—I'll call her "Jane." It wasn't just her sharp, stylish yet professional outfit that caught attention; it was the quiet confidence she carried, even in a room full of skeptics. As the only woman in the room, she knew the stakes were high, but she was ready to take on whatever came her way.

The crux of this encounter lay not in proving Jane's worth superficially but in demonstrating the undeniable power of expertise and self-belief. Armed with extensive industry experience, a portfolio of successful leadership initiatives, and a treasure trove of data-driven insights, she was ready to shift perceptions. Her opening remarks emphasized her profound understanding of the current market dynamics, introducing innovative strategies poised to capture untapped business growth areas. With each point, Jane meticulously wove in evidence of her expansive career, not as a boast but as a testament to her capability and foresight. Addressing the elephant in the room—*her singular position in a traditionally male-dominated setting*—she leveraged studies and real-world examples that focus on the critical importance of diversity in thought and leadership. Through her eloquence and meticulous analysis, she unraveled the fabric of unconscious bias, presenting a compelling case for a more inclusive approach to decision-making.

Challenges were met not with defensiveness but with adaptability, showcasing a solution-oriented mindset that further instilled confidence in her abilities. Jane's call for open dialogue, coupled with an encouragement of feedback, nurtured a collaborative environment. No longer were voices overshadowed; instead, they were elevated, contributing to *a richer, more diverse conversation.* The emotional landscape of the room was palpably transformed throughout the discourse. Initial skepticism morphed into respect and admiration for her undeniable expertise and the respectful, inclusive manner in which she navigated the discussion. The gravity of her success in such an environment resonated deeply, serving as a potent reminder of the barriers that continued to erode in the face of determination and knowledge.

The realization dawned collectively—the importance of challenging and overcoming ingrained biases, not as an act of defiance but as a pathway towards enriched perspectives and innovation in leadership and decision-making. This encounter wasn't just about breaking down the barriers for Jane; it served as a trumpet-like call to others, inspiring a wave of change through the simple yet profound act of understanding and embracing diversity.

As the discussion continued, Jane shared her insights on the power of diverse perspectives in problem-solving and decision-making. She emphasized the value of actively seeking out differing viewpoints and incorporating them into the decision-making process. Her words were met with nods of agreement and renewed determination to create a more inclusive environment for all. The conversation shifted towards actionable steps that could be taken to promote diversity and inclusion within their organization. Some ideas included creating mentorship programs, hosting diversity workshops, and implementing blind hiring practices. Throughout it all, Jane remained a humble yet powerful presence, guiding the group towards tangible solutions while also acknowledging that change would not happen overnight. But as she so eloquently put it,

*"Every step we take towards inclusivity is a step towards
a better and brighter future for us all."*

—Jane

The meeting concluded with a renewed sense of purpose and hope. Jane's wisdom and leadership had left a lasting impact on everyone in the room, inspiring them to continue striving for a more inclusive and diverse workplace. As they closed their laptops and prepared to leave, they knew that this was just the beginning of their journey towards creating positive change. As the days went by, the team put their plans into action, with Jane's guidance and support. Slowly but surely, they began to see changes within their organization—more diverse hires, improved communication between different teams, and an overall shift in company culture towards one of inclusivity.

Challenge biases with confidence and knowledge.

In recounting this narrative, the message is clear—empowerment stems from believing in one's capabilities and confronting challenges head-on with knowledge and grace. It's a testament to the enduring strength of diversity in fostering not only a more inclusive world but a smarter, more insightful one at that. Every space we occupy, every room we enter, presents an opportunity to rewrite the script, to transform skepticism into respect, and to *lead by example*. To those standing at the doorway of their own challenging encounters, the path forward is paved with bricks of self-belief, expertise, and the unwavering courage to challenge the status quo. Together, we can turn the tide, one empowering encounter at a time.

Game-Changing Meeting: A Lesson in Empathy and Inclusivity

In the realm of business, it's easy to get caught up in numbers, targets, and the bottom line. But sometimes, it takes just one meeting, one voice, to pivot the entire course of a marketing strategy—*for the better*. This recollection is the story of what started as a regular day in our marketing team and ended up being a turning point for our company's brand—a moment that shifted us towards a more inclusive and empathetic way of connecting with our audience.

The day kicked off like any other. The usual hustle, the pre-meeting chatter, and a packed agenda for our branding session. Same room, same faces, but there was this buzz in the air—like something big was about to happen. And as we got into the meeting, it became pretty clear: we *were* onto something special.

A colleague of ours—a woman whose voice, often drowned out in the corporate noise, was about to change everything. With a mix of nerves and determination, she shared her insights. But instead of stats or charts, she told a story that hit home for everyone in the room. She shined a light on something we'd been missing: the huge, untapped potential of the underrepresented female market. She didn't just talk about their purchasing power—she showed us their need for brands that connect with them *on a deeper level*.

Her words were a wake-up call. We instantly realized our narrative was missing something big—empathy. That moment sparked a shift in how we saw things. We stopped thinking of our audience as just consumers and started seeing them as people with unique stories and experiences. It was a powerful moment, not just for our purpose but for our connection as a team.

Inspired by the courage and insight we had just witnessed, we decided it was time to rethink our marketing strategy. Instead of focusing solely on our products, we shifted to telling stories—real stories about the experiences, dreams, and challenges of our audience. Inclusivity became the heart of our brand, and we started connecting with more people by sharing authentic, relatable narratives. The results? Incredible. Customer loyalty and engagement went through the roof, far beyond what we expected. But the real win was the feedback. Customers told us they felt seen, heard, and understood—maybe for the first time by a company of our size in the industry.

This wasn't just a strategy shift; it was a powerful lesson in empathy, diversity, and the importance of listening to voices that often go unheard. It showed us that meaningful change can start with something as simple as listening and valuing different perspectives.

I'm sharing this because it's not just about what we accomplished—it's about showing others what's possible. Take a moment to think about your own approach. How could embracing diversity and leading with empathy change the way you connect with your audience? The truth is, it's not just about keeping up with change—it's about creating it. Listen, learn, and let diverse perspectives guide you. You might just be amazed at the transformation that follows.

The biggest lesson from this experience? Building real connections and lasting customer loyalty starts with empathy and inclusivity. When we embrace diverse perspectives in our strategies, we don't just reach more people—we create deeper, more meaningful connections with everyone our brand touches. This isn't just the future of marketing—it's a reflection of genuine care and the drive to make a meaningful impact.

Inspirational Women

The narratives of Audrey Hepburn, Katie Diasti, and Kamala Harris illuminate this chapter, offering rich insight into the journeys of these remarkable leaders. Each story pinpoints different aspects of overcoming barriers, from Audrey's strategic humanitarian work and Sandberg's advocacy for women in leadership roles to Harris's groundbreaking ascent in the historically male-dominated legislative industry.

A Case Study of Timeless Motivation and Creativity

Audrey Hepburn's remarkable life spanned across the gleaming screens of Hollywood to the far-flung corners of the world as a dedicated humanitarian. Her story is not just a tale of glamor and fame but a profound lesson in resilience, compassion, and timeless style that continues to inspire individuals and professionals alike.

Key Achievements and Contributions

Audrey Hepburn's illustrious acting career was adorned with numerous awards, including an Academy Award for Best Actress, setting her apart as a true icon of the silver screen. However, her legacy extends far beyond her cinematic achievements. Hepburn became a global fashion emblem, her sense of style epitomizing elegance and sophistication, influencing the fashion industry and public alike even years after her prime.

Perhaps her most profound contribution was her humanitarian work. Serving as a UNICEF Goodwill Ambassador, Hepburn dedicated her later years to advocating for children in need across developing countries. Her efforts were recognized globally, culminating in the awarding of the Presidential Medal of Freedom—one of the highest civilian awards in the United States.

Her Character and Values

Hepburn's character was shaped significantly by her experiences during her childhood in Nazi-occupied Holland, fostering a deep compassion within her for those suffering. This empathy was evident in her hands-on approach to humanitarian work, choosing simple over luxury to stay connected with those she aimed to help.

Humility, kindness, and generosity were her distinguishing traits, making Hepburn not just a beloved actress and style icon, but a cherished colleague and friend to those who knew her personally.

Her Legacy and Influence

Audrey Hepburn's impact stretches far beyond the realms of entertainment and fashion. She set a benchmark for celebrity activism, encouraging public figures to leverage their influence for social good. Her dedication to children's rights and education has left a lasting impression, continuing to benefit global initiatives focused on childhood development in impoverished regions. Organizations founded in Hepburn's honor perpetuate her philanthropic legacy, ensuring her values endure, uplifting lives even decades after her passing.

Let's face it. Who hasn't seen that unmistakable outline of Audrey Hepburn, striking a pose with her trademark elongated cigarette holder and little black dress? It's practically a universal signal for chic and timeless elegance. From movie posters to fashion inspiration boards, Audrey's iconic image has become a symbol of grace, style, and sophistication that continues to influence trends even today.

Inspirational Quotes

Her words embody her belief in possibility, happiness, and the power of altruism. They continue to inspire and resonate, offering timeless wisdom.

"Nothing is impossible, the word itself says 'I'm possible!"

—Audrey Hepburn

"The most important thing is to enjoy your life–to be happy–it's all that matters."

—Audrey Hepburn

"As you grow older, you will discover that you have two hands, one for helping yourself, the other for helping others."

—Audrey Hepburn

Connecting to Her Audience

Audrey Hepburn's extraordinary life and legacy offer a wealth of inspiration for all of us looking to make a meaningful mark on the world, blending professional success with personal integrity and a commitment to making the world a better place. Thus, reminding us of the importance of resilience, the impact of serving others, and the power of maintaining grace and elegance in personal and professional endeavors. Her story encourages us to examine how we might overcome our own challenges with the same determination, contributing positively to the broader community, and defining our personal brand in a way that reflects timelessness and authenticity.

Reflective Questions For You, the Reader

1. Consider how Audrey Hepburn's resilience can inspire you to face current challenges. What lessons can you draw from her determination?

2. Reflect on how you can use your talents and position to impact your community positively. How might Hepburn's commitment to philanthropy in unexplored industries influence your actions?

3. Think about how elegance and grace can play a role in your personal and professional image. What aspects of Hepburn's style can you incorporate into your brand?

***

The Inspirational Journey of Katie Diasti

In the typically conventional and laden with taboos domain of
menstrual care, Katie Diasti stands out as a shining example
of innovation, sustainability, and empowerment. Through her
visionary leadership and dedication, she founded Viv Period
Care, a company that has rapidly evolved from a promising
startup to a pioneering force in the sphere of menstrual health.
Diasti's remarkable journey with Viv Period Care, from its
initial conception to its rise as a trailblazer, not only defines her
entrepreneurial spirit but also her commitment to community
building and addressing the often overlooked needs within
traditional markets. Her work in creating eco-friendly and
accessible menstrual products offers profound examples into the
challenges and triumphs of entrepreneurship, the importance of
building supportive communities, and the impactful results of
addressing unmet needs in long-established industries.

Innovating Menstrual Care

Katie Diasti set out on her entrepreneurial journey fueled by
a clear and compelling vision: to completely transform the
menstrual product industry by introducing sustainable and
convenient options. Driven by a personal epiphany about the

significant environmental impact and widespread dissatisfaction
with conventional menstrual products among women, she aimed
to make a change. Observing that many women were seeking
alternatives that were both eco-friendly and user-friendly, Katie
saw an opportunity to innovate.

Key Achievements and Contributions

Katie's entrepreneurial spirit and dedication to sustainability have
led to several key achievements and contributions in the menstrual
product industry. Some of her notable accomplishments include:

Development of eco-friendly materials

Katie recognized the harmful environmental effects caused by
traditional disposable menstrual products, which often end up in
landfills or oceans. In response, she worked tirelessly with her team
to develop sustainable materials for their products. These include
biodegradable cotton, organic bamboo, and reusable silicone.

Introduction of innovative designs

With a focus on user-friendliness, Katie has introduced
revolutionary designs that have made period care more convenient
and comfortable for women. This includes period panties
with built-in absorbent layers, menstrual cups with leak-proof
technology, and washable cloth pads that can be reused for up to
3 years.

Empowering women through education

Along with providing eco-friendly and innovative products, Katie is also passionate about educating women on the importance of sustainable period care. She has conducted workshops and seminars in schools and communities, spreading awareness about the harmful effects of traditional menstrual products on the environment.

Collaboration with NGOs

In order to reach a wider audience and make a bigger impact, Katie has partnered with various non-governmental organizations (NGOs) that focus on environmental sustainability and women's health. Through these collaborations, she has been able to distribute her products to underprivileged communities and provide them with access to safe and environmentally-friendly period care through these key initiatives.

—**Launch of Viv Period Care** with a focus on sustainability and user experience.

—**Securing over three million in funding** validating the market's need for innovative period care solutions.

—**Development of an interactive mobile app** enhancing the customer experience with technology.

—**Cultivation of a vibrant social media community**

—**Recognition with prestigious accolades**, including being named in Forbes 30 Under 30 in Retail & E-commerce.

Thus, Viv Period Care was born, with Katie at the helm, steering the company towards creating eco-friendly menstrual products that not only reduce waste but also provide a high level of comfort and reliability. Under her leadership, Viv Period Care has not only introduced a range of sustainable menstrual products but also launched a pioneering mobile app. This app is a game-changer in menstrual health management, offering users the ability to track their menstrual health and receive personalized recommendations, thus enhancing the overall user experience and promoting better menstrual health awareness. Through her innovative approach, Katie Diasti is redefining menstrual care, making it more sustainable, convenient, and aligned with the needs of modern women.

Disrupting an Industry

Viv Period Care has not only established new standards for product quality and sustainability in the menstrual care industry but has also sparked a much-needed broader conversation about menstrual health and environmental awareness. By adopting a holistic approach that combines superior quality menstrual products with cutting-edge technology and vigorous community engagement, Viv has significantly reshaped consumer expectations, setting new trends within the industry. Their commitment to eco-friendliness and fostering open discussions about menstrual health challenges the status quo, encouraging other brands to follow suit and prioritize both sustainability and the well-being of their consumers. This strategic blend of innovation, environmental consciousness, and community support positions Viv Period Care as a trailblazer, influencing not just market dynamics but also contributing to a more informed and eco-conscious society.

Business Impact

There has been a noticeable shift in consumer behavior towards sustainable menstrual products. More individuals are seeking eco-friendly options, driving demand for products that are both effective and environmentally conscious. Conversations around menstrual health are evolving, leading to a breakthrough in how the topic is addressed. This change is fostering a more supportive and informed community, breaking down stigma and encouraging open dialogue. The industry is also undergoing a reevaluation of its standards, with many competitors expanding their offerings to meet the growing demand for diverse and inclusive products. There has been a significant boost in investment interest towards innovations in women's health and wellness, signaling a promising future for advancements in this space.

Testimonials Echoing Change

The impact of Viv Period Care transcends beyond its product offerings into fostering a deep sense of trust and loyalty among its users and observers alike.

Feedback from a thrilled customer Viv Period Care has revolutionized their menstruation experience, signifying the superior quality of their products. Alongside their intuitive app, which plays a crucial role in demystifying menstrual health, customers have found a newfound appreciation for managing their menstrual cycle with ease and comfort. This positive transformation stands as a testament to Viv's commitment to enhancing the well-being of individuals during their period.

An industry expert highly praised Katie for her innovative approach, recognizing her visionary integration of sustainability, technology, and community efforts. By doing so, Katie has managed to empower women and redefine the conversations around menstruation, setting a new standard for how society approaches this topic. This acknowledgment is a testament to Katie's significant contribution to promoting a more inclusive and environmentally conscious discussion in this field.

A well-known health and wellness blogger gave high praise to Viv, acknowledging its unparalleled innovation in both product design and technology within the menstrual product industry. They wrote about how Viv stands out for its commitment to improving user experience and pushing the boundaries of what's possible in personal care. These glowing testimonials give legitimacy to Viv's profound impact in fostering a healthier, more sustainable, and inclusive dialogue surrounding menstruation. By challenging existing stigmas and promoting open discussion, Viv is at the forefront of transforming societal perceptions, making it easier for everyone to engage in conversations about menstrual health without fear or embarrassment.

A Blueprint for Future Entrepreneurs

Katie Diasti's story with Viv Period Care stands as an emblem of entrepreneurial grit, innovation, and commitment to making a difference. The key takeaways from this narrative highlight the importance of addressing overlooked consumer needs, the power of community and education in brand building, and the critical role of technology in enhancing user experiences.

Katie's voyage is a testament to the fact that with a clear vision, persistent effort, and an unwavering commitment to values, it is possible to challenge norms and bring about meaningful change. Viv Period Care is not just a success story in the realm of menstrual products; it is a clarion call for future entrepreneurs to pursue ventures that contribute to societal well-being, sustainability, and the empowerment of underserved communities. Katie Diasti and Viv Period Care remind us all that the path to disrupting industries and touching lives begins with a simple yet profound step: addressing the unmet needs with courage, innovation, and an unwavering belief in one's vision.

Reflective Questions For You, the Reader

- Consider your own core values and beliefs. How can you infuse them into your work and purpose?

- What are some ways in which you can challenge norms and bring about meaningful change in your community or industry?

- How can persistent effort and a strong commitment to values help in achieving success and making a positive impact for your business or position?

- In what ways does Viv Period Care's story inspire you to think differently about innovating and making a difference?

Shattering Ceilings, Building Bridges

In the rich landscape of American politics, few narratives resonate with the depth and significance of Kamala Harris's journey. Her historic rise to the Vice Presidency of the United States has shattered numerous glass ceilings, setting unprecedented milestones. Not only is she the first woman to ever hold this esteemed office, but she also stands as the first Black and first South

Asian American to achieve this high honor. The significance of Harris's accomplishments extends far beyond personal triumph; her story serves as a radiant symbol of hope, symbolizing the profound impact of resilience, representation, and reform focusing on the evolving dynamics of American political and social landscapes, providing inspiration to countless individuals who see in her a reflection of their potential and a reaffirmation of the American promise that every dream is within reach.

Early Life and Career

Born to immigrant parents—a mother hailing from India and a father originating from Jamaica, Kamala Harris' early life in Oakland, California, was deeply influenced by a strong consciousness of civil rights and a commitment to public service. As a proud alumnus of Howard University, an institution known for fostering future leaders in the African American community, and a graduate of the University of California, Hastings College of the Law, Harris began her remarkable career with a solid foundation in law and justice.

Her journey through the legal and political landscape of California was marked by a series of groundbreaking 'firsts'. Starting her career as the district attorney of San Francisco, Harris demonstrated an unyielding commitment to justice and an innovative approach to tackling crime. Her achievements and leadership in this role paved the way for her election as the Attorney General of California, where she made history as the first woman of color to hold this prestigious position. In these roles, Harris was known for her tough yet fair approach to law enforcement, focusing on reformative measures and the importance of community engagement.

Harris' ascension from district attorney to Attorney General of California was not just a personal victory but a true example of hope and inspiration for many, laying the groundwork for what would be a trailblazing path to the Vice Presidency of the United States. Her journey from the courtroom to the corridors of political power in Washington, D.C., has been emblematic of her resilience, dedication to justice, and the pioneering spirit that has characterized her career. As the Vice President, Harris continues to break barriers, embodying the aspirations of immigrants and people of color across the nation and around the world.

Path to the Vice Presidency

Harris' bid for the Vice Presidency was deeply rooted in a career-long dedication to justice, equality, and the improvement of her community. Throughout her distinguished career, she consistently advocated for the underserved and marginalized, striving to make a tangible impact on society. Her campaigns managed to resonate with millions of Americans by championing critical issues such as vast criminal justice reform, the urgent need for affordable housing, and the accessibility of healthcare for all individuals. Harris' unwavering commitment to these principles helped to define her political journey, setting her apart as a fervent advocate for change and progress within the American political landscape.

Key Achievements and Impact

Each step of Harris' career has been marked with substantive achievements and impactful initiatives. As Attorney General of California, she fought for homeowners against big banks, securing a twenty billion settlement that benefitted tens of thousands of families at risk of foreclosure. In the Senate, Harris introduced the LIFT, the Middle Class Act, striving to provide tax relief for working and middle-class families, and co-sponsored the Dream Act, which sought to provide a pathway to citizenship for undocumented immigrants who came to the U.S. as children.

However, her most profound influence might stem from shattering glass ceilings, but building the bridge of inspiration for the forthcoming generations is her true heroism. In her Vice Presidential acceptance speech, she poignantly remarked

> *"I may be the first, but I won't be the last."*
> —Kamala Harris

A statement that resonates deeply with both a sense of responsibility and a spark of hope. This declaration not only reflects on her historic achievement but also underlines her dedication to paving the way for future leaders, ensuring that her trailblazing path will be followed by many more to come.

Challenges Faced

Harris' trailblazing journey to prominence was marked by significant challenges. Subjected to intense scrutiny under the glaring national political spotlight, she encountered numerous obstacles including harsh criticisms and deeply ingrained biases. Despite these hurdles, Harris navigated her path with exceptional grace and unwavering determination, characteristics that she continues to exhibit to this day. Her relentless perseverance in the face of adversity has not only been a defining aspect of her illustrious career but has also laid a solid foundation for future generations of women leaders to follow. Beyond her personal achievements, Harris tirelessly works towards creating a more equitable and just society. Leveraging her influential platform, she consistently strives to amplify the voices of those marginalized by systemic inequalities while pushing for compelling systemic change. Her efforts are geared towards dismantling barriers and fostering an environment where equal opportunities are accessible to all, reflecting her deep commitment to social justice and equity.

Legacy and Future Impact

Kamala Harris' political legacy is still unfolding at the time of this writing, yet her influence is already indelible. Her ascent to the Vice Presidency has redefined what's possible for women, particularly women of color, in political leadership roles across sectors. Her advocacy work and policy initiatives continue to shape a more equitable society. And her example of empathy, adaptability, and empowerment serves as a guiding light for all individuals seeking to build their personal brands with purpose and impact.

Her story has ignited a spark among women from all walks of life, especially those in leadership, business, and entrepreneurial roles—inspiring them to break their own ceilings, build their own bridges, and contribute to a legacy of change.

Kamala Harris embodies the essence of American possibilities for women. Her dedication to breaking barriers, coupled with her commitment to public service, offers a compelling blueprint for leadership that transcends gender and race. For women in leadership, women in business, and new women entrepreneurs, Harris' journey is a testament to the power of perseverance, the importance of representation, and the impact of leaving doors open for those who follow. This is her continuing legacy—a bridge to a future where the seats at the table of power reflect the diversity and potential of humanity itself. In the words shared during a visit to a local organization, Kamala Harris inspired young girls to

> *"Dream with ambition, lead with conviction, and see yourself in a way that others may not, simply because they've never seen it before."*
>
> —Kamala Harris

It's a powerful reminder of the role models needed to shape a more inclusive and equitable world and Harris stands at the forefront of this monumental shift.

Aim High and Never Quit

Through her groundbreaking achievements, Kamala Harris has paved the way for marginalized communities to see themselves represented in positions of power. Her continued presence and dedication to creating a better future for all is a testament to the importance of representation and the impact it can have on generations to come. As we continue to strive towards a more diverse and inclusive society, let us remember the words of Harris to "see ourselves in a way that others may not" and use our unique perspectives and experiences to make positive change. Let us also keep doors open for those who follow, knowing that their success only strengthens our collective progress as a society. With Harris as an example, we can dream with ambition, lead with conviction, and work towards a future where everyone has the opportunity to reach their full potential. So let us continue to write our own stories and pave the way for those who come after us, just as Harris has done for all of us.

Reflective Questions For You, the Reader

- Consider your own experiences and how they have shaped your perspective. How can you use those unique insights to contribute to a more inclusive society?

- Are there any barriers that you have faced or are currently facing in pursuing your ambitions? How can we work together to break down these obstacles for future generations?

- In what ways can we actively support and uplift each other, as Harris has done, in order to create a stronger and more empathetic community?

- What small steps can you take today to help pave the way for a more equitable and diverse world tomorrow?

Strategies for Overcoming Obstacles

Some of these strategies include education and awareness, active allyship, and creating inclusive spaces. By educating ourselves and others on issues of diversity and inclusion, we can become better equipped to recognize and challenge discrimination when we encounter it. Additionally, being an active ally means taking tangible actions to support marginalized communities and speaking up against injustice.

Creating inclusive spaces is also crucial in breaking down barriers. This includes promoting diverse representation in all industries and ensuring that everyone feels welcome and valued in their workplaces, schools, and communities. By actively supporting and uplifting each other, we can create a stronger sense of community where everyone's voices are heard.

But change doesn't happen overnight. It takes consistent effort from individuals to make a difference. You are probably wondering *"what small steps can I take today?"* Well, it can start with educating yourself and others about systemic oppression and privilege. This could be through reading books or articles, attending workshops or seminars, or simply having open and honest discussions with friends and family.

Actively listen: This technique will help you amplify the voices of marginalized groups. This means giving them space to speak and sharing their stories to a wider audience. It also means using your own connections to advocate for those without a voice.

Be an ally: It requires recognizing when you make mistakes and being willing to learn from them. No one is perfect in this journey towards equity and inclusion, but acknowledging your privileges, biases, and blind spots is an essential part of growth. By continuously educating yourself and taking action, you can become a better ally and contribute to creating a more just society.

Use your platform: Support organizations and movements that are fighting against oppression and working towards social justice. Things like donating money or resources, volunteering your time, or using your voice to raise awareness. Remember that being an ally is an ongoing process and it requires consistent effort and self-reflection. Together, we can work towards building a more equitable world for everyone.

Build a Strong Support Network: The critical role of mentors, peers, and sponsors in offering guidance, support, and advocacy is truly indispensable. These relationships not only help you navigate the challenges of professional and personal growth but also open doors to new opportunities. Surrounding oneself with a robust network can significantly impact one's success and well-being, offering a foundation of encouragement and insight that is invaluable.

Continuous Learning and Skill Development: Actively engaging in ongoing education and enhancing one's skill set places you at the forefront of industry trends, technological advancements, and modern leadership practices. This not only ensures competitiveness in a rapidly evolving market but also primes you for seizing upcoming opportunities with confidence and expertise.

Personal Branding: Articulating and showcasing your unique value and expertise is not just about self-promotion. It's a strategic approach to opening new doors and establishing credibility within professional circles. By effectively communicating what sets you apart, you can make a memorable impact and foster opportunities for advancement and collaboration.

Assertiveness and Collaboration: Asserting your ideas confidently and effectively, while also being open and receptive to feedback, strikes a fundamental balance crucial for effective leadership and fostering innovation. This approach not only ensures that diverse ideas are heard and considered, but it also promotes a culture of respect and cooperation, essential for driving forward-thinking solutions and advancements.

Create Leadership Opportunities: Actively seeking and creating opportunities to take on leadership roles not only enhances your skills but also significantly increases visibility among decision-makers. This proactive approach can lead to recognition of your capabilities and potential for future leadership positions.

Growth Mindset: Embracing challenges as opportunities for personal and professional development, rather than obstacles, cultivates resilience and adaptability. These are essential traits for successfully navigating the complex and often unpredictable landscape of the business world. Adopting a growth mindset encourages continuous learning and improvement, enabling you to thrive in dynamic environments.

We now have a comprehensive toolkit of effective strategies to help dismantle common barriers. These strategies include setting achievable goals, seeking out resources and support, embracing mistakes as learning opportunities, practicing self-compassion, and maintaining a positive outlook. By utilizing these tools and adopting a growth mindset, you can overcome challenges and setbacks to ultimately reach their full potential. However, it is important to recognize that this level of development does not occur in isolation. Collaboration and teamwork are also crucial components of personal growth and success in business. Working with others allows for diverse perspectives and skills to be combined, leading to innovative solutions and increased productivity.

It's also essential to prioritize self-care while on the journey of development. Taking breaks, engaging in hobbies or activities outside of work, and practicing mindfulness can all contribute to overall well-being and resilience. This has been a lifelong challenge for me. I've always been the type to hunker down and power through, but I'm now learning to find a healthier balance.

Key Takeaways and Concluding Thoughts

To cultivate a learning and supportive community, this chapter wraps up with questions designed to spark deeper conversations about overcoming obstacles. These inquiries encourage readers to reflect on their personal challenges, promote the value of support networks, understand tactics for navigating systemic hurdles, and consider how personal branding and a growth mindset can be instrumental in overcoming professional challenges.

With engaging stories and thoughtful analysis, this chapter doesn't just mention the barriers women encounter in the business world; it seeks to empower readers with confidence and drive. My goal is to light a fire in you, my beloved sister, motivating you to carve your own path, advocate for yourself and others, and see barriers not as obstructions but as opportunities for reaching new heights.

This chapter reiterated that although barriers exist, they can be overcome through resilience, strategic action, and a truly supportive community. I leave you, the reader, with the empowering reminder that by breaking these barriers, women pave the way for future generations of leaders to thrive and shape a more inclusive business and political landscape. So let's continue to break boundaries, challenge limitations, build bridges, and ultimately, rewrite the narrative of women in business. This is an exciting time and our journey has just begun. See you in the next chapter!

Reflective Questions For You, the Reader

- Can you recall a moment in your career when you faced a challenge and struggled to find a way to overcome it? How did you ultimately navigate the situation, and what lessons did you learn from the experience?

- Who are some role models or mentors that have helped guide you through challenges in your professional life? How did they support and encourage you to persevere and overcome obstacles?

- What steps do you take to continuously develop your skills and stay ahead in your field? Are there any resources or strategies that have been particularly helpful for you?

- How do you articulate and showcase your unique value

and expertise in a professional setting? Do you have any tips for building a strong personal brand?

- In what ways do collaboration and assertiveness play into your leadership style? Can you think of an example where balancing these traits was crucial for achieving success?

3

The Power of Storytelling

In today's fast-paced digital age, we are bombarded with information from all directions. It is easy to become overwhelmed and desensitized to the constant stream of news, advertisements, and social media updates. But amidst this chaos, storytelling remains a powerful tool to cut through the noise and connect with others on a deeper level.

From the ancient oral traditions passed down by generations to modern forms of media like books, movies, and podcasts, storytelling has always been a fundamental part of human communication. It allows us to share our experiences, beliefs, and emotions in a way that is relatable and engaging.

But beyond simply entertaining or informing, storytelling also has the ability to shape our perceptions and understanding of the world around us. Through our brand stories, we can challenge societal norms, break down barriers, and inspire *real change.*

By defining these key themes, we can weave together insightful case studies with personal anecdotes to awaken the transformative power of storytelling and arm ourselves with these essential tools for lifelong success.

Strength

In the realm of human connection, few tools are as powerful and as profoundly impactful as storytelling. It has the unparalleled ability to foster empathy, fuel resilience, and ignite our imaginations, bridging worlds and experiences far beyond our own. And for women in business, storytelling can be a game-changer.

As we continue to navigate the often tumultuous and male-dominated corporate world, we must remember the power of our own stories. Each and every one of us has a unique journey, filled with triumphs and challenges that have shaped us into the leaders we are today. But too often, we shy away from sharing our stories. We fear being judged or not taken seriously. We worry that our experiences may not be seen as valuable or relevant in the competitive business arena.

Here's the truth: ***Our stories hold incredible value.*** They allow us to connect with others on a deeper level, to inspire new perspectives and spark meaningful change. Sharing our struggles and triumphs reveals our vulnerability—A trait we will come to understand is not a weakness, but rather a profound source of strength.

Empathy

At its core, empathy is about understanding and sharing the feelings of others. Storytelling invites us into the lives of characters, real or imagined, allowing us to experience their joys, challenges, and pain as if they were our own. The *Humans of New York* project masterfully encapsulates this concept, presenting personal narratives that resonate with readers worldwide, building bridges of empathy one story at a time. By immersing ourselves in the stories of others, we open our hearts and minds to diverse perspectives, fostering understanding and connection.

My personal voyage into storytelling began with an empathy-driven narrative inspired by a childhood friend's nightmare with bullying. This anecdote serves as a notable recognition of the power of empathy in storytelling—how sharing our stories can provide solace, understanding, and connection. For a brand, empathy-driven storytelling is not only a powerful tool to foster customer loyalty but also a reflection of its values and commitment to a more inclusive world.

From the very beginning, my passion for storytelling has been intertwined with a deep sense of empathy—a lesson learned not in the quiet confines of libraries, but in the raucous halls of my elementary school. It was there, amid childhood's cacophony, that I bore witness to the struggle of my close friend under the crushing weight of consistent bullying. This experience, painful yet profound, became the bedrock of my narrative ethos.

The echoes of whispered taunts and the silent retreats to lonely corners were etched into my young mind, painting a stark, poignant picture of my friend's daily reality. Witnessing her battle with exclusion, physical violence, and ridicule carved a deep well of empathy within me—one that overflowed into every story I would come to tell. This isn't merely about recounting tales; it is about weaving communications of understanding and connection, about turning the microphone back to those whose voices had been drowned out by cruelty, it's about protecting the ones we love.

The emotional landslide of watching someone you care about grappling with such pain leaves you forever changed. It compels a young heart to grow vast in its capacity for compassion, and instills an unwavering commitment to wield storytelling as a balm for wounded souls. My friend's ordeal became a reason for most of my many pursuits, guiding me towards stories that do more than entertain, they resonate deeply and open our eyes—they heal.

This transformation was not immediate; it has been a voyage. A voyage that has taught me the irreplaceable value of empathy in storytelling. That the act of sharing stories rooted in our most vulnerable experiences can stir a profound sense of solidarity and understanding. It reminded me that at our core, we all seek to be seen, to be understood, and to know we're not alone in our battles.

Today, I stand by the belief that integrating empathy into storytelling is not only beneficial, it's imperative. For brands and individuals alike, it represents a commitment to a world where every story is honored, every struggle acknowledged. Empathy-driven storytelling transcends mere transactional interaction; it builds bridges, fostering a community rooted in understanding and mutual respect.

My friend's remarkable resilience in the face of adversity, coupled with the transformative power of sharing her personal journey, has served as a focus of inspiration in my branding voyage. Witnessing her courage and the way she navigated through challenges with grace over the years stands as a powerful monument to the resilience and strength of the human spirit. It also highlighted the profound impact that empathy and understanding can have on individuals and communities. This invaluable lesson, learned so many years ago, has not only enriched my perspective but continues to fuel my passion and drive my storytelling mission forward, reminding me of the profound connections and transformations that can arise from genuine narratives.

By sharing our stories with one another, we do more than merely enrich our personal experiences; we also reach out and touch the hearts of others in profound ways. When we share these stories, we create ripples of empathy and understanding, forming a powerful current that eventually reshapes the world around us. By supporting the mission of inclusive storytelling, you're playing a pivotal role in building a more empathetic and connected world.

Resilience

Resilience, the capability to overcome adversity, is both a theme within and a product of storytelling. The case study of Malala Yousafzai powerfully demonstrates this, detailing her unwavering advocacy for girls' education despite formidable challenges. Through her story, we see the impact of personal narratives in mobilizing global movements and building resilience across communities.

A Beacon of Resilience and Hope for Education

In the face of extreme adversity, there are those rare, resilient souls who not only manage to survive but also shine a brighter light, illuminating a path in guidance and inspiration for others to follow. Among these exceptional individuals, Malala Yousafzai stands out as a towering testament to what indomitable courage, unwavering determination, and the transformative power of education can achieve. Despite facing life-threatening challenges, Malala's steadfast commitment to advocating for girls' education around the world has not only earned her the Nobel Peace Prize at just 17 years old, but has also sparked a global movement, encouraging millions to stand up for the right to education and equality. Her story is a powerful reminder of how one voice can inspire change and make a significant impact in the world.

The Incarnation of Her Resilience

On what appeared to be a typical day in 2012, Malala Yousafzai's life was forever altered in a dramatic and violent manner when she was shot in the head by a Taliban gunman. The reason for this brutal attack was her fearless and outspoken advocacy for girls' education in her native Pakistan–a stance that challenged the oppressive policies of the Taliban. Despite the dire circumstances of this attack, which could have easily broken a lesser spirit, Malala's response was nothing short of remarkable. She did not emerge as a victim; instead, she became an even stronger advocate for educational rights, transforming into a global symbol for the fight against educational inequality. Her miraculous recovery and her powerful speech at the United Nations less than a year after the attack not only hardened her already extraordinary resilience but also amplified her message, inspiring millions around the world to stand up for the right to education for all children, regardless of gender.

Inspiring Global Action through Advocacy

Malala Yousafzai's influence stretches well beyond her own story of courage and resilience. Through her visionary initiative, the Malala Fund, she has become a global champion for the right to education for girls in developing countries. This noble cause seeks to dismantle the systemic barriers that prevent girls from accessing quality education. The Malala Fund's mission is to empower girls by advocating for policy changes, investing in local education leaders, and supporting innovative education projects across the globe.

To date, the fund's remarkable efforts have reached over 130 million girls, providing them not just with hope, but with real opportunities to learn and grow. This is achieved through strategic advocacy for policy shifts that prioritize girls' education and substantial investments in programs that are designed to have a deep impact on local communities.

An exemplary initiative of the Malala Fund is the 'Gulmakai Network' named after Malala's pseudonym when she wrote a blog about life under the Taliban. This network focuses on supporting education champions in countries like Afghanistan, Pakistan, Lebanon, Turkey, and Nigeria. Thanks to this network, more than 100,000 girls have received substantial support, enabling them to attend school, pursue their educational goals, and dream of a brighter future.

Malala's own efforts to speak out on international platforms have significantly contributed to increasing global awareness about the importance of education for girls. Her powerful advocacy has played a pivotal role in mobilizing resources and increasing funding for primary education in developing countries. The tangible impact of her work is evident in the heightened global commitment to ensuring that girls everywhere can access the education they deserve. Through the collective actions inspired by Malala's leadership, there's a growing optimism that the barriers to girls' education can be overcome, transforming the lives of millions around the world.

An Unquenchable Thirst for Knowledge

Despite her global influence and the fact that she has become a symbol of the fight for education and women's rights worldwide, at her core, Malala Yousafzai remains a dedicated student, deeply committed to learning. After the assassination attempt on her by the Taliban, her insistence on receiving books and continuing her lessons even while hospitalized in a critical condition, demonstrates her unwavering belief in the transformative power of education. This determination not just to survive but to continue her education underlines the importance she places on learning as a tool for change. Her graduation from Oxford University in 2020, where she earned a degree in Philosophy, Politics, and Economics, serves as a potent reminder and a powerful symbol of her message; that education is an inalienable right that should be afforded to all, regardless of gender, socio-economic background, or geographical location. Her journey from a young girl fighting for her right to go to school in the Swat Valley of Pakistan to a graduate of one of the world's leading universities embodies her conviction that education can uplift individuals and transform societies.

The Power of One Voice

Malala Yousafzai's resilience transcends merely surviving a brutal assassination attempt by the Taliban; it's epitomized in her unwavering dedication to championing educational rights in the face of persistent threats. Her courage and resolve are encapsulated in her inspiring words.

> *"When the whole world is silent, even one voice becomes powerful."*
>
> —Malala Yousafzai

This statement is not just a testament to her own strength but a call to action that has resonated globally. Through her actions and eloquent speeches, Malala has not just fought for her own right to education but has sparked a global movement, encouraging millions around the world to stand up not only for their own rights but also for the rights of others. Her story is one of remarkable bravery and an enduring commitment to education and equality, making her a symbol of hope and the power of peaceful activism.

Legacy of a Fighter

Malala Yousafzai transcends her identity as merely a survivor of a violent attempt on her life. She embodies the relentless struggle for education and gender equality, demonstrating unwavering courage in the face of adversity. Rather than allowing fear to silence her, Malala leverages her global platform to champion the rights of millions of girls who are systematically denied education due to a confluence of social, economic, and political barriers.

Her narrative is not solely one of survival against the odds; it is a powerful testament to the capacity of the human spirit to seek empowerment through education. Malala's journey serves as a call of incitement, stirring individuals and communities worldwide into action, aiming to dismantle the barriers to education for all children, regardless of gender. She encourages us to look beyond our limitations and strive for a world where every girl can dream of and achieve a brighter future.

By fearlessly advocating for the cause of education in the midst of personal risk and sacrifice, Malala illustrates poignantly that even from the depths of despair and oppression, powerful and transformative change can emerge. Malala's steadfast commitment to education and equality continues to ignite movements for change, proving that one voice, no matter how young or seemingly alone, can indeed echo around the world, stirring consciences and effecting meaningful progress.

A Personal Echo

In her own words, Malala does not wish to be remembered as the girl who was shot by the Taliban but as *the girl who fought for education*. This distinction is crucial; it reframes her story from one of victimhood to one of empowerment, a narrative that encourages us to challenge injustices and fight for what is right.

Parallelly, my own story of navigating difficult times with resilience has taught me the importance of perseverance, self-reflection, and staying focused on long-term goals. Through sharing this narrative, I highlighted the role of storytelling in not just overcoming challenges but in transforming them into opportunities for growth and empowerment. This is the essence of resilience—harnessing our stories to create positive change and navigate through life's obstacles.

Innovation

In the realm of animation, Pixar stands as a true testament of creativity, innovation, and unparalleled storytelling. From revolutionizing the animation industry with *Toy Story* to tugging at heartstrings with *Up,* Pixar's films have consistently captured the imagination of audiences worldwide. This case study explores the ethos driving Pixar's success, dissecting the company's commitment to creativity, leadership in storytelling, technological advancements, and the synergistic power of collaboration.

Storytelling Prowess

Since its establishment, Pixar Animation Studios has become a household name, renowned for its groundbreaking animation techniques and compelling storytelling that resonates deeply with audiences of all ages, from children to adults. What distinguishes Pixar as a leader among animation studios is not solely its cutting-edge technology or superb animation quality. It's the heart and soul poured into every film—the intricate stories, the rich, multi-dimensional characters, and the emotional depth that each movie offers. Pixar's commitment to storytelling is evident in its ability to create worlds and narratives that captivate viewers, making us laugh, cry, and reflect. This unique blend of technological innovation and storytelling excellence is what propels Pixar beyond its peers, securing its place as a leader in the animation industry.

Creativity and Innovation

At the core of Pixar's philosophy is a relentless pursuit of creativity and innovation. This is evident from its very first feature film, *Toy Story*, which ushered in a new era of computer-animated feature films. Pixar's culture encourages risk-taking, experimentation, and the belief that creativity springs from collaboration among individuals from diverse backgrounds. The studio's open, collaborative environment ensures that the most captivating ideas always bubble to the surface.

Toy Story, which hit the theaters in 1995, wasn't merely a technological marvel for being the pioneering feature-length film crafted entirely with computer animation; it also drastically raised the bar for storytelling within the animation genre, establishing a new standard that many films strive for but few achieve. This groundbreaking film not only demonstrated Pixar's unmatched commitment to creating deeply immersive, meticulously detailed worlds but also to populating these worlds with vibrant, dynamic characters that could resonate with and captivate audiences of all ages. The characters' rich narratives and emotional depth allowed viewers to form lasting connections, making *Toy Story* more than just a movie, but a cherished part of many childhoods and adult lives alike.

It marked a pivotal moment in cinematic history, proving conclusively that animated films could carry the same emotional weight and narrative complexity as their live-action counterparts. This was a revelation that challenged preconceived notions about animation being a genre primarily for children. *Toy Story* opened the door to a new era of animated storytelling, inspiring a generation of filmmakers to discover the potential of animation in telling diverse, sophisticated stories. Its success paved the way for countless other animated films that seek to enchant and engage, demonstrating the limitless possibilities of animation in capturing the human experience.

Leadership and Emotional Storytelling

Pixar's unparalleled storytelling magic isn't just a product of its innovative animation techniques but is deeply intertwined with its leadership's forward-thinking vision. This vision places a high value on establishing an emotional connection with the audience, considering it paramount above all else. This unique approach is evident in Pixar's films, such as *The Incredibles*, which masterfully blend thrilling action, sharp humor, and profound emotional truths in a way that few others can.

The Incredibles is more than just an animated film; it's a deep look into the complexities of family dynamics, the importance of individuality, and the struggles of balancing personal desires with familial responsibilities. It captivates viewers of all ages, leaving a lasting impact on its audience through its exploration of these universal themes. The movie showcases Pixar's ability to create rich, multidimensional characters that audiences can relate to and root for, adding to its enduring appeal. Indeed, Pixar has masterfully branded each of its characters, ensuring they stand out as memorable and distinct. Through innovative design and storytelling, Pixar has created a universe of characters that resonate deeply with audiences of all ages, making each character's journey unique and unforgettable.

Through its compelling narratives, memorable characters, and a steadfast commitment to quality, Pixar continues to set the standard for animated films. The studio proves time and again that stories with heart and depth, stories that express the emotional spectrum of the human experience, can resonate universally. Pixar's films remind us of the power of the imagination to connect, inspire, and entertain, leaving a lasting mark on the hearts and minds of viewers around the world.

Case Example: *Inside Out*

Inside Out is not just a film; it's a masterfully crafted cinematic journey that takes audiences on an unforgettable emotional adventure. Diving deep into the intricate interplay of emotions residing within a young girl's mind, it navigates the complex challenges of growing up with an unprecedented depth of insight and compassion. This exceptional piece of cinema stands as a shining testament to Pixar's groundbreaking approach to storytelling and animation, which skillfully brings to life the abstract concepts of human emotions in ways that are both vibrantly colorful and profoundly compelling.

Through its innovative narrative, *Inside Out* explores the nuanced spectrum of joy, sadness, anger, fear, and disgust, presenting a rich canvas of the human emotional experience. It does so through the lens of a young girl's journey towards understanding and acceptance of her complex feelings, making it resonate deeply with audiences across the globe. By collaborating closely with psychologists and neuroscientists, the filmmakers were able to lend an impressive level of authenticity and psychological depth to the depiction of the emotional turmoil and triumphs experienced by the characters, making each moment on screen feel incredibly real and touching.

The meticulous attention to emotional detail and the commitment to accurately portraying the inner workings of the mind have resulted in a film that is not only a visual spectacle but also a deeply resonant experience for viewers of all ages. *Inside Out* thereby becomes a vivid exploration of the ways in which emotions influence our memories, decisions, and personal growth, offering both entertainment and enlightenment to its audience.

The innovative storytelling and stunning depth of research combined make *Inside Out* a remarkable film that celebrates the full spectrum of emotions and the important role they play in shaping our lives. It is a heartfelt reminder of the versatility and talent of Pixar's team, who can turn a complex concept into an engaging, accessible story that captures the imagination of both children and adults alike. *Inside Out* is truly a masterpiece that stands out as one of the most significant animated films of its time, offering experiences and delights that linger long after the credits roll. As long as they continue to create films that touch our hearts and minds, their legacy will live on.

Technology and Adaptation

Pixar's pioneering spirit stands out remarkably, especially in its groundbreaking use of technology in animation. With the debut of each new film, Pixar doesn't just inch past the existing limits of what's technologically feasible; it leaps forward, redefining those boundaries entirely and setting unprecedented standards for the entire industry to follow. This unwavering commitment to technological innovation ensures that their narratives are not merely told but are vividly brought to life through visually stunning animations that captivate and enchant audiences across the globe.

This relentless pursuit of excellence in blending storytelling with cutting-edge technology has not only cemented Pixar's reputation as a vanguard in the realm of animation but has also continually pushed the envelope, challenging and expanding the very possibilities of storytelling through film. Each project undertaken by Pixar serves as a testament to their philosophy of blending art with technology, thereby creating immersive experiences that resonate with viewers of all ages, making them a beloved fixture in homes around the world. This approach has not only garnered critical acclaim but has also ensured that Pixar remains at the forefront of the animation industry, continually inspiring both creators and audiences with its innovative visions and storytelling prowess.

Case Example: *Finding Nemo*

Finding Nemo not only captivated audiences worldwide with its emotionally rich narrative and endearing characters but also showcased unparalleled underwater environments. These breathtaking scenes were the result of years of technological advancements in animation, setting a new benchmark in the industry. The film's vivid depiction of oceanic landscapes, brimming with a kaleidoscope of vibrant marine life and intricate ecosystems, marked a significant milestone in the evolution of animation history. It wasn't just about the visual feast; the film demonstrated Pixar's unwavering commitment to pushing the boundaries of what is technically and artistically possible, immersing viewers in ever-more detailed and dynamic worlds that stretch far beyond the limits of our imagination. This dedication to innovation and meticulous attention to detail has not only set a new standard for animated films but has also made *Finding Nemo* a touchstone for future projects in the realm of animation and beyond. Pixar's efforts in creating such a masterpiece demonstrate the studio's role as a pioneer, continually advancing the medium and inspiring both filmmakers and audiences with the limitless possibilities of storytelling.

In addition to technological advancements, *Finding Nemo* also exemplifies Pixar's unique approach of blending relatable themes with vibrant characters and awe-inspiring visuals. The story's central theme of family, resilience, and the power of love resonated deeply with viewers, making it one of Pixar's most beloved films. By grounding their stories in universal emotions and experiences, they have been able to create a lasting impact, transcending generations and cultures. This approach is a testament to Pixar's understanding of the universal human experience and their ability to translate it into compelling narratives that touch the hearts of audiences worldwide.

Through *Toy Story, The Incredibles, Inside Out and Finding Nemo*, Pixar has continually demonstrated its mastery in blending cutting-edge technology with powerful storytelling, pushing the boundaries of what is possible and captivating viewers with their imaginative and emotionally resonant worlds. As they continue to pave the way for future generations of storytellers, Pixar's legacy will undoubtedly endure, inspiring and delighting audiences for years to come. So, it can be said that Pixar has not only revolutionized the animation industry but has also left an indelible mark on the history of storytelling, showcasing the power and beauty that can be achieved by combining art with technology. As we eagerly await their future projects, we can only imagine what new worlds and stories Pixar will unveil, continuing to inspire and enchant us with their unparalleled creativity and innovation. In this way, Pixar has firmly established itself as a trailblazer in the world of animation, and its impact will continue to be felt for generations to come.

Collaboration and Cross-Disciplinary Work

At the core of Pixar's remarkable success is a strong emphasis on collaboration. This iconic animation studio has fostered a culture that prioritizes the sharing of ideas across different departments, encouraging constant communication and the exchange of creative insights. By actively seeking input from various disciplines, Pixar ensures that a diverse range of perspectives contribute to the storytelling process, significantly enhancing the richness and depth of its films. This collaborative approach has not only led to groundbreaking innovations in animation but has also resulted in a beloved and critically acclaimed body of work that resonates with audiences around the globe. Pixar places great emphasis on emotional connection in their films. They understand that audiences are looking for more than just entertainment; they want to be moved emotionally.

Pixar's story is one of daring dreams, imaginative storytelling, and the incessant pursuit of excellence. The studio's focus on creativity, innovation, leadership in emotional storytelling, technological prowess, and collaboration has not only set it apart but also significantly influenced the animation industry and creative culture at large.

For aspiring filmmakers, creative professionals, and business leaders, Pixar's model offers profound lessons in fostering a culture of innovation, the importance of emotional connection, and the power of collaborative creativity. In reflecting on Pixar's story, we are reminded of the boundless potential of storytelling when coupled with vision and collective genius.

One of the key elements of Pixar's success is their dedication to creating a culture of innovation. From its inception, the company was built on a foundation of risk-taking and pushing boundaries. This mindset allowed for groundbreaking animated films that continuously pushed the limits of technology and storytelling. For aspiring filmmakers, this serves as a reminder to embrace failure, take risks, and constantly challenge themselves in order to reach new levels of creativity.

Imagination

Imagination lies at the heart of storytelling, enabling the crafting of worlds that extend far beyond the confines of our reality. Pixar's storytelling prowess exemplifies this, creating characters and narratives that resonate across age groups, fueled by imagination and the universal truths embedded within their tales.

This case study offered a glimpse into the Pixar universe where futures are imagined, cultures are influenced, and storytelling knows no bounds—illustrating how the concept of 'Branding Like A Girl' harnesses creativity and emotional connection to make a lasting impact. As we peek behind the curtain of Pixar, we can understand how their unique approach to storytelling and branding has shaped their success and impacted the creative landscape.

Key Takeaways and Concluding Thoughts

Throughout this chapter, we've traversed the realms of strength, empathy, resilience, and innovation, exploring their critical roles in storytelling. From the intricate human recollection of a victim of a schoolyard bully to the resilient voice of Malala Yousafzai, and the imaginative wonders of Pixar, we've seen how storytelling can transcend simple entertainment to become a force for understanding, change, connection, and an *unforgettable experience*.

As we wrap up this chapter, consider stories that have moved you, changed you, or inspired you personally. Reflect on how you can wield the power of storytelling to impact others. In sharing our experiences, we not only enrich our own lives but also contribute to a more empathetic, resilient, and imaginative world. So the next time you sit down to write, remember that your words have the power to create a lasting impact. Use them wisely and tell the stories that need to be told.

Whether it's through highlighting social issues in a film or using personal anecdotes to spark conversations about important topics, storytelling has the power to influence and motivate people. As individuals, we all have our own unique stories to tell. And by sharing them with others, we not only connect on a deeper level but also remind ourselves of our common humanity. *Storytelling brings people together.*

Let's come together to share, listen, and grow through the stories that unite us all. **#TellYourTale**

Reflective Questions For You, the Reader

- How can storytelling amplify the core values of Branding Like A Girl?

- In what ways does sharing personal experiences contribute to building a more empathetic and resilient brand image?

- How can the philosophy of Brand Like A Girl leverage the power of storytelling to create a more imaginative and inclusive narrative?

4

The Power of Us

I n the rapidly evolving landscape of modern business, where change is the only constant, the clamor for a more inclusive approach to leadership has never been louder. Now we will uncover the essence and unprecedented benefits of collaborative leadership, a paradigm shift that interweaves the collective intelligence and capabilities of individuals to achieve common goals. We'll explore the theory's foundation, offer practical advice to foster collaboration, and illuminate the concept with compelling case studies from the Open Source Movement, Toyota Production System, and The Gates Foundation.

The Essence of Collaborative Leadership

At its core, collaborative leadership is rooted in the understanding that there is tremendous potential inherent within groups, and it seeks to harness this collective power to achieve objectives that far surpass what any individual could achieve on their own. This approach is deeply grounded in the principles of trust, respect, and the free exchange of ideas, creating an environment where every team member feels valued and empowered. In a collaborative leadership model, leaders act more as facilitators or guides, rather than traditional authoritative figures or dictators. They work to bring out the best in their teams by encouraging open communication, fostering a sense of community, and promoting the sharing of diverse perspectives. The goal is to build a cohesive unit that can navigate challenges more effectively and innovate solutions that are richer and more valuable than the sum of its parts. Brené Brown perfectly encapsulates the essence of effective leadership with her insightful assertion.

> *"A leader is anyone who takes responsibility for recognizing the potential in people and ideas and has the courage to develop that potential."*
> —Brené Brown

This profound statement deeply resonates with the core principle of collaborative leadership, which significantly transcends the traditional notion of leadership being about merely giving orders or directing actions. Instead, it pivots towards the more inspiring and empowering task of nurturing and unlocking the hidden talents and possibilities within others. This nuanced approach to leadership greatly emphasizes the importance of building meaningful relationships, fostering a culture brimming with trust and respect, and vigorously encouraging innovation and creativity.

Such a leadership style is deeply rooted in the belief in the power of collective intelligence and the invaluable contribution of every individual towards achieving common goals. It champions the idea that true leadership is not about holding a position of power but about empowering others to realize their full potential. This paradigm shift key points the significance of emotional intelligence, empathy, and the ability to inspire and motivate. By creating an environment where individuals feel valued and understood, a leader can harness the diverse strengths and perspectives of their team, leading to more innovative solutions and better outcomes.

In essence, this approach to leadership is not just about achieving targets or milestones; it's about creating a legacy of empowerment, where each team member is encouraged to grow, contribute, and make a difference. It's a testament to the power of recognizing and nurturing potential, leading with courage, and the transformative impact it can have on organizations and society at large.

Cultivating Collaboration: A Practical Guide

How do we construct these dynamic teams and organizations that are capable of adapting and thriving in an ever-changing environment? The process involves a significant transition that encompasses both philosophical and practical changes. It requires a profound shift in mindset towards embracing flexibility, fostering innovation, and encouraging collaboration among all members. This mental transformation is pivotal for cultivating an adaptive and resilient organizational culture.

On a practical level, tangible actions are equally important. Implementing new team structures that are more agile and less hierarchical can significantly enhance responsiveness and creativity. Encouraging open communication across all levels of the organization is essential for breaking down silos and facilitating the free flow of ideas. Fostering a culture of continuous learning and improvement is crucial. This can be achieved by providing ongoing educational opportunities, promoting a mindset of curiosity, and encouraging the exploration of new ideas and approaches.

This dual approach, combining both a philosophical shift and practical actions, ensures that the organization is not only well-equipped to navigate current challenges but is also poised for future success. It creates a foundation for building teams and organizations that are resilient, innovative, and capable of continuous evolution.

Fostering Open Communication

It is crucial to actively encourage the sharing of ideas, opinions, and feedback among all team members. This can be achieved by creating a supportive environment where transparency and open dialogue are highly valued. Fostering an atmosphere of trust is indispensable in effective collaboration, as it allows team members to feel safe and respected when voicing their thoughts and suggestions. Such an approach not only significantly enhances team dynamics by preventing misunderstandings and conflicts but also leads to the development of more innovative and creative solutions. By leveraging the diverse perspectives and expertise within the team, a culture of open communication can drive the team towards achieving exceptional results.

Promoting Diversity and Inclusion

Actively building teams that celebrate diversity is essential in today's globalized world. It brings a wealth of varied perspectives, crucial for fostering innovation and creativity in any organization. Diversity encompasses a range of human differences, including but not limited to race, ethnicity, gender, age, social class, physical ability, and religious beliefs. By committing to inclusivity, we ensure that every voice, regardless of background or identity, is heard and valued. This approach not only enriches the team's dynamics by incorporating a wide array of viewpoints but also leads to more effective and innovative solutions. Drawing from a broad spectrum of ideas and experiences allows for a more comprehensive understanding of challenges and opportunities, ultimately resulting in better decision-making and problem-solving. Fostering an inclusive environment where everyone feels welcome and valued can significantly enhance employee engagement, satisfaction, and retention. In turn, organizations become more attractive to a diverse talent pool, further perpetuating the cycle of innovation and creativity.

Empowering Teams

To truly elevate team performance and achieve remarkable outcomes, it's imperative to provide teams with the autonomy they require over their tasks and projects. Granting this level of empowerment fosters a profound sense of accountability and motivates each member to take full ownership of their contributions. This approach not only serves as a powerful motivator, inspiring individuals to dedicate their utmost effort and apply their unique skills, but also significantly enhances team dynamics and productivity. By valuing and trusting in their capabilities, you instill a culture of responsibility, innovation, and creativity. This leads to the development of innovative solutions that can tackle complex problems in new and efficient ways. Such an environment supports a stronger, more cohesive team, where members feel valued, motivated, and connected to their work and to each other. Investing in team empowerment sets a foundation for a thriving, innovative, and engaged workforce, capable of achieving beyond conventional limits.

Real-World Triumphs of Collaborative Leadership

Open Source Movement

The Open Source Movement, led by innovative visionaries such as Linus Torvalds, the mastermind behind Linux, and Jimmy Wales, the co-founder of Wikipedia, stands as a testament to what collective effort can achieve. It is a movement that truly showcases the power of collaboration and shared knowledge. At its heart, the movement is built on a profound belief that the collective wisdom of many surpasses the knowledge of the individual. This foundational principle has spurred the development of groundbreaking platforms that have significantly altered the technology and information landscape, making it vastly more accessible to people around the globe.

The inception of Linux by Linus Torvalds brought forth an operating system that was not only free but also customizable by anyone with the skills to do so, encouraging innovation and personalization. Similarly, Wikipedia, under the guidance of Jimmy Wales, became a monumental repository of human knowledge, freely accessible and editable by users worldwide, reflecting a diverse range of perspectives.

These platforms, among countless others inspired by the open source philosophy, have not merely facilitated technological advancements and creative endeavors. They have been instrumental in democratizing access to technology and information, thereby contributing to a more equitable society. By allowing free access and the ability to modify and distribute, open source projects have eliminated barriers to entry for technology creation and use. This has enabled a more diverse group of people to contribute to and benefit from technological progress, ensuring that the tools and information necessary for innovation are not confined to a privileged few but are available to all.

Through the power of collaboration, the Open Source Movement continues to foster innovation, stimulate creativity, and play a pivotal role in making technology and information accessible to everyone. It champions the idea that by working together, sharing ideas, and building upon each other's work, the global community can overcome challenges and create solutions that benefit humanity as a whole.

Toyota Production System

Toyota's extraordinary success story is largely due to its groundbreaking approach to production, which is deeply ingrained in the principles of teamwork, continuous improvement, and mutual respect among all levels of employees. This pioneering production model, famously known as the Toyota Production System (TPS), has not only catapulted Toyota to a leading position in the global automotive industry but has also given rise to an entire philosophy centered around lean manufacturing techniques. The TPS emphasizes eliminating waste, optimizing processes, and engaging all employees in problem-solving, thereby ensuring quality and efficiency at every stage of production.

This approach has had a profound impact, inspiring an array of industries worldwide to adopt lean manufacturing principles. Companies across sectors have seen the value in adopting a collaborative leadership style and fostering a culture where continuous improvement is not just encouraged but is a shared responsibility among all members of the organization. This has led to significant enhancements in product quality, customer satisfaction, and operational efficiency.

The influence of Toyota's methodologies extends well beyond the realm of manufacturing. Businesses in services, healthcare, and technology, among others, have adopted lean principles to streamline their operations, reduce costs, and improve their overall performance. By focusing on value creation and waste elimination, organizations are able to respond more quickly to customer needs and market changes, driving innovation and excellence.

In essence, Toyota's revolutionary approach has not only redefined the standards of automotive manufacturing but has also inspired a global movement towards leaner, more efficient, and more responsive business models. The legacy of the Toyota Production System is a testament to the power of visionary leadership and the transformative impact of adopting a culture of continuous improvement and respect for all people and their collaborative ideas.

The Gates Foundation

The Gates Foundation stands as an exemplary example of how collaborative leadership can address complex global challenges effectively and efficiently. By forming strategic partnerships across a diverse range of sectors, including governments, nonprofit organizations, and the private sector, the Foundation not only showcases the power of collective efforts but also sets a new standard for philanthropy. These partnerships extend beyond the mere sharing of resources; they are about leveraging and combining different perspectives, expertise, and capabilities to foster innovation and develop sustainable solutions to some of the world's most pressing issues.

This approach of working together, pooling resources, knowledge, and strengths, significantly amplifies the impact of their initiatives, achieving remarkable results that would be utterly impossible for any single entity to accomplish on its own. From improving global health and education to increasing access to information technology and combating climate change, the Gates Foundation's model demonstrates the incredible potential that lies in unity. It proves that when diverse groups come together, united by a common vision and driven by a shared goal, the potential for positive change is not just immense—it's virtually boundless.

The Gates Foundation's strategy emphasizes the importance of transparency, accountability, and mutual respect among all partners, ensuring that every stakeholder has a voice in the decision-making process. This inclusive approach not only fosters a stronger sense of commitment and ownership among the involved parties but also ensures that the devised solutions are more holistic and effectively address the needs of those they aim to help.

By championing such a collaborative model, the Gates Foundation inspires other organizations and individuals to consider how they, too, can contribute to global betterment through partnership and cooperation. It communicates the message that in our interconnected world, complex problems require multifaceted, cooperative solutions—and that together, we can achieve far more than we ever could alone. The Gates Foundation's work is a powerful reminder of the boundless potential that collaborative effort holds for creating a better, more equitable world for future generations.

Personal Insights and Reflections

During my tenure as a team leader, I have come to the profound realization that adopting a collaborative leadership style has not only led to exceptional results in terms of project success but has also significantly enhanced team morale. This particular approach centered around creating an inclusive environment that championed open dialogue. By doing so, each team member felt their voice was heard and their contributions valued, fostering a sense of belonging and appreciation.

I made it a priority to acknowledge individual efforts on a daily basis, thereby reinforcing their importance to our collective achievements. This practice ensured that every team member felt integral to our shared successes, boosting their motivation and commitment to our objectives.

By choosing to face challenges as a unified front, we unlocked our collective creative potential. This collaborative problem-solving approach allowed us to devise innovative solutions and adapt to changes more swiftly and effectively. It was this mindset of unity and mutual respect that transformed our team into a resilient and innovative force, one that was perfectly equipped with the skills and mindset necessary to surpass even our most ambitious goals.

This journey of collaboration taught me invaluable lessons about the strength of collective effort. It underlined the remarkable fact that when individuals come together, united by a common vision and purpose, they have the power to achieve extraordinary feats. Through this experience, I learned the true essence and power of working together towards a common goal, proving beyond a doubt that a collective effort can indeed lead to exceptional and unprecedented achievements. As a leader, I am committed to continuing to foster and cultivate a collaborative culture that prioritizes respect, inclusivity, and continuous learning. After all, as the saying goes, 'If you want to go fast, go alone. If you want to go far, go together.' By embracing this philosophy, organizations can not only achieve great success but also create a better future for all. So, let us all be inspired by the examples of Toyota and the Gates

Foundation and strive to collaborate, innovate, and drive positive change in our own spheres of influence. Together, we can truly make a difference.

Key Takeaways and Concluding Thoughts

This is a call to action for us all to engage in a larger conversation about the transformative power of collaborative leadership. Your story, whether it's about a small win or a major breakthrough, could inspire others to seek out new ways of leading and working together. Let's come together to build a treasure trove of knowledge that can help guide us toward achieving greater success through the power of unity and shared vision.

Collaborative leadership is not merely a trend but a profound evolution in the way we conceive of and enact leadership. It invites us to rethink hierarchies, value diversity, and harness the collective strength of our teams and organizations. Simon Sinek reminds us,

> *"Leadership is not about being in charge. It's about taking care of those in your charge."*
>
> —Simon Sinek

With collaborative leadership, we embody this principle, forging ahead into a future where success is a shared achievement, reflecting the collective efforts, dreams, and aspirations of all involved. May this chapter be a stepping stone towards that future, one where collaborative leadership lights the way to unprecedented possibilities and achievements.

Reflective Questions For You, the Reader

- How could the principles of collaborative leadership, which emphasize shared goals, open communication, and mutual respect, completely transform the operational dynamics of your team or even your entire organization? Consider the potential shifts in creativity, productivity, and overall morale that could arise from embracing a more inclusive and participatory approach to leadership.

- Have you personally experienced scenarios where actively choosing to embrace collaboration led to outcomes that not only met but significantly surpassed your initial expectations?

- I strongly encourage you not to keep these lessons to yourself. Instead, why not share your unique stories and reflections with a wider audience?

5

The Future is Female

In this crucial chapter, we will hone in on the intricacies of the evolving business landscape, a domain that is slowly but surely shifting towards a more inclusive and equitable environment. This transformative shift not only recognizes but also ardently celebrates the significant contributions of women leaders and entrepreneurs, marking a pivotal moment in history. What were once mere ripples of change in the fabric of the business world have now turned into powerful waves. These waves are carving out spaces that were once rigid and monolithic, transforming them into dynamic forums brimming with innovation, leadership, and undeniably, female prowess. This new era in business is not just about acknowledging the presence of women in the boardroom or in leadership roles; it's about valuing their insights, embracing their unique perspectives, and leveraging their skills for the greater good of organizations and society at large. As we are reminded of these developments, it becomes clear that the journey towards gender equality in the business realm is not only about breaking barriers but also about building bridges—bridges that lead to a more diverse, vibrant, and *successful* future.

The 21st century marks the dawn of a promising era for women in the realm of business, signaling a significant departure from a time when gender often predetermined one's position and opportunities within the corporate hierarchy. No longer are we confined to the archaic norms that once dictated the professional landscape; instead, today we find ourselves on the brink of a revolutionary shift, observing with keen interest as women are not merely participants but are at the forefront, leading and fundamentally altering the contours of the business world.

Let's look at the essence of this unprecedented transformation, illuminating the growing recognition and appreciation of women's contributions across various sectors. It highlights the breakthroughs and challenges, narrating stories of resilience, innovation, and leadership that underline the pivotal role women are playing in shaping the future of business.

Overview of Gender Equality in Business

The journey towards achieving gender equality in the workplace has been an arduous and challenging one, marked by numerous obstacles along the way. However, through relentless perseverance and determination, there have been significant shifts toward a more equitable working environment. These changes have been brought about by a combination of policy reforms aimed at creating equal opportunities, improvements in corporate governance to ensure fair treatment and representation, and a noticeable shift in societal perceptions towards gender roles. Such transformations pave the way for a more gender-inclusive business environment, where talents and skills are valued regardless of gender.

Women are increasingly assuming pivotal leadership positions across a diverse range of rapidly growing sectors, including tech startups, sustainable enterprises, political seats, and many more. This detailed exploration peers into the myriad of opportunities now accessible to women, who are actively dismantling long-standing barriers in industries previously dominated by male leadership. By taking on these influential roles, women are making substantial contributions to enriching workforce diversity, while simultaneously carving out innovative and entrepreneurial pathways.

Future Trends in Female Entrepreneurship and Leadership

In stepping into leadership roles, women are not merely participants but are establishing themselves as formidable key players and visionaries. They bring unique perspectives that are essential for driving transformative change within the

global business ecosystem. Their involvement is fostering an
environment ripe for innovation, where fresh ideas are not only
welcomed but are also instrumental in shaping the future of
businesses.

This significant shift in the professional landscape marks a
progressive evolution, underlining the indispensable role that
women play in propelling growth, fostering creativity, and
ensuring sustainability in today's economy. By breaking through
the glass ceiling, women leaders are setting new benchmarks
for success, demonstrating that diversity in leadership not only
enhances the quality of decision-making but also contributes to a
more inclusive and equitable business world.

As this trend continues, it's becoming clear that the impact
of women in leadership extends far beyond individual sectors,
influencing broader societal shifts towards gender equality
and empowerment. The rise of women in leadership roles
is a testament to their resilience, ingenuity, and the critical
contribution they make in driving forward a more dynamic and
diverse global business landscape.

What does the future hold for women in business? The essence
here is not just to chart a course but to inspire action and resilience.
As we move towards a future where gender diversity is not just
a goal but the norm, there will be even more opportunities for
women to take on leadership positions and shape the direction of
industries.

Already, we are seeing positive changes with more companies actively seeking out diverse perspectives and promoting women into executive roles. From tech giants like IBM and Google to traditional corporations such as General Motors and Coca-Cola, businesses are recognizing the value of having women in top leadership positions. This shift also extends beyond the corporate world, with governments around the world implementing policies to increase gender diversity in leadership roles.

But despite these advancements, there is still work to be done. The representation of women in leadership positions remains low compared to men, particularly when it comes to women from marginalized or underrepresented communities. This is not only a gender issue, but also an intersectional issue that affects women of color, LGBTQ+ individuals, and those with disabilities.

To continue making progress towards true diversity and inclusivity in all industries, it is important for companies to actively promote and support women from all backgrounds into leadership positions. This can include implementing mentorship programs, providing equal opportunities for career advancement, and creating inclusive company cultures that value diverse perspectives.

Companies must also address the systemic barriers that may prevent women from reaching leadership roles. This includes addressing unconscious biases in hiring processes, offering flexible work arrangements to accommodate caregiving responsibilities, and closing the gender pay gap.

By creating an environment where women are given equal opportunities to succeed and thrive in leadership positions, companies can benefit from diverse perspectives and experiences.

Katrina Lake and Stitch Fix: Pioneering the Future of Retail and Tech

Katrina Lake, with her groundbreaking vision and remarkable tenacity, stands tall in the shifting dynamics of leadership within the fast-paced realms of the retail and technology industries. As the visionary founder and CEO of Stitch Fix, Lake has not merely catapulted her company into the spotlight; she has also broken through historical barriers by becoming the first woman to take a tech company public in the U.S., challenging and changing the status quo.

This case study takes us deeply into Lake's entrepreneurial journey, from her initial conception of Stitch Fix to its rise as a powerhouse in personalized fashion. It cements her pivotal role in transforming the industry through innovative technology and customer-centric business models. By examining her strategic approaches to overcoming obstacles, fostering a culture of innovation, and her ability to anticipate and adapt to market trends, the study showcases the intricacies of her leadership style.

It also sheds light on the challenges Lake faced, from securing initial funding in a male-dominated venture capital world to navigating the complexities of scaling a tech business. Her story is a testament to resilience, showing how she overcame skepticism and setbacks with her unwavering determination and a keen focus on long-term vision.

Lake's significant contribution goes beyond her company's success; she is actively shaping the narrative that the 'future is female,' inspiring a new generation of female leaders in technology and beyond. Through her journey, we gain a profound understanding of the qualities essential for transformative leadership, such as visionary thinking, resilience, and the ability to foster innovation.

Katrina Lake's story is not just about building a successful company; it's about redefining leadership and showing that visionary leaders can indeed reshape entire industries. Her achievements serve as a powerful example of how persistence, innovation, and a commitment to breaking down barriers can lead to monumental shifts in the business landscape, making her a role model for aspiring leaders everywhere.

Background and Education

Growing up in a highly competitive environment, Lake developed a keen passion for innovation and entrepreneurship from an unusually early age. This wasn't just a fleeting interest; it was a

profound fascination that became the driving force behind her
academic pursuits and future career choices.

At the prestigious Stanford University, she didn't just attend;
she excelled academically. Lake dove deeply into the realms
of economics and business, subjects that fascinated her. Her
dedication and inquisitive nature allowed her to develop complex
theories and practical applications, laying a robust and solid
groundwork for her future endeavors. Stanford was more than a
university for Lake; it was a launchpad that propelled her into the
realms of innovation and business strategy.

Seeking to further her excellence and deepen her understanding,
Lake pursued an MBA at the world-renowned Harvard Business
School. This was no small feat. The advanced education
she received there was transformative, providing her with a
comprehensive understanding of business dynamics, economic
strategies, and the subtleties of leadership in a global context.
Harvard didn't just fortify her foundational knowledge; it
expanded her horizons and refined her analytical skills, preparing
her to navigate the complex business world.

These educational experiences were not merely academic
milestones; they deeply shaped her perspective and approach
towards the business world. Through her rigorous academic
training, Lake's skills into the retail and tech industries were
sharpened like never before. With a keen eye for untapped
potential and market inefficiencies, she identified a unique market

opportunity that stood out from the rest, one that others had overlooked.

This unique blend of a competitive upbringing, stellar academic achievements, and a strong foundation in economics and business strategy set the stage for Lake to make a significant impact in the retail and tech industries. Leveraging her unique insights, innovative approach, and the ability to identify and exploit niche markets, Lake was poised to carve out a new niche in the market, one that could potentially redefine industry standards and consumer expectations.

In essence, Lake's journey from a curious child in a competitive environment to a pioneering figure in the business world is a testament to the power of education, determination, and the relentless pursuit of innovation. Her story is one of inspiration, demonstrating how a blend of academic excellence, practical experience, and strategic insight can lead to groundbreaking success in today's fast-paced and ever-evolving business landscape.

Founding Stitch Fix

In 2011, during a time when the e-commerce landscape was undergoing rapid changes and evolution, entrepreneur Katrina Lake keenly observed a significant gap in the retail market. Traditional brick-and-mortar stores offered a tactile, in-person shopping experience, but lacked the convenience and efficiency that the burgeoning online shopping platforms were beginning to provide. On the other hand, these online platforms, while convenient, failed to replicate the personalized service and experience offered by physical stores. Recognizing a substantial opportunity in these observations, Katrina Lake took the innovative step of founding Stitch Fix. This groundbreaking company introduced an unprecedented personalized styling service, a concept that was novel at the time.

Stitch Fix's service was ingeniously designed to blend the advanced capabilities of data science with the human touch and discerning eye of professional fashion stylists. By doing so, it managed to curate highly personalized selections of clothing and accessories that precisely matched the individual tastes, sizes, and style preferences of its customers. These selections were then delivered directly to the customers' homes, providing a tailored shopping experience that seamlessly filled the void between impersonal online shopping and the traditional retail experience.

This tailor-made approach not only catered to a diverse array of women's fashion needs with remarkable precision but also pioneered a revolutionary approach in the retail industry. It successfully melded technology with a personal touch in a way that had never been seen before, setting a new standard for the retail sector. Stitch Fix's innovative business model has had a profound influence on the evolution of the retail sector, inspiring other companies and setting a new benchmark for personalized online shopping experiences. Its success has demonstrated the value and appeal of combining technological innovation with personalized service, reshaping the way consumers think about and engage with e-commerce and retail shopping.

Key Achievements

Under the visionary leadership of Katrina Lake, Stitch Fix expanded swiftly, transforming from a promising startup into a major player in the retail industry, and ultimately reaching a significant milestone with a successful public offering in 2017. This achievement was not solely a personal triumph for Lake but also represented a monumental advancement for women in the realms of technology and business. It demonstrated the crucial role that women can assume in steering companies towards remarkable achievements, showcasing that female leadership is not only vital but instrumental in shaping the future of industries.

The IPO of Stitch Fix served as a compelling testament to the power of female leadership in catalyzing substantial market disruption and fostering innovation. This was a notable moment in the industry where the impact of women in leadership positions began to be truly recognized and celebrated, breaking traditional barriers and setting new benchmarks for what is achievable. It proved the unique perspectives and strategies that women bring to the table, which in many cases lead to fresh and transformative approaches to business and technology.

This event not only mounted the success of Stitch Fix but also set a precedent for what women-led enterprises are capable of achieving in the competitive business landscape. It opened doors for future female entrepreneurs and executives, inspiring a new generation of women to aspire to leadership roles within their respective fields. The success of Stitch Fix under Lake's leadership exemplifies how embracing diversity at the highest levels of management can lead to extraordinary outcomes, encouraging the industry to reevaluate and expand the opportunities for women in leadership roles.

Thus, the Stitch Fix IPO not only marked a personal victory for Katrina Lake and a breakthrough for Stitch Fix as a company but also shone a spotlight on the broader significance of female leadership in driving innovation and achieving success in today's business world. It stands as a path to progress, emphasizing the critical importance of inclusivity and diversity in creating more dynamic, competitive, and innovative businesses.

Impact on the Industry

Under the visionary leadership of Katrina Lake, Stitch Fix has not only revolutionized the way we perceive the intersection of retail and technology, but it has also left a profound impact on the broader landscape of these industries. The company's success story is not just about its financial achievements but also about how it has ignited a much-needed dialogue around the necessity of diversity in leadership roles. This is particularly significant in sectors that have been traditionally dominated by male leaders, where Stitch Fix's influence has been transformative.

Personal and Professional Influence

The company's unparalleled success under Lake's guidance has served as a catalyst, encouraging and inspiring a substantial increase in female entrepreneurship across various sectors. It demonstrates the untapped potential of women to lead and innovate, reshaping industries with fresh ideas and approaches. Lake's journey from the inception of Stitch Fix to steering it towards becoming a towering example of success drives home the critical importance of creating and maintaining an inclusive environment where diverse leadership can thrive.

Such an environment not only paves the way for women leaders to emerge and flourish but also enables them to leave a significant mark on the future of their industries. Through her remarkable achievements, Katrina Lake has showcased that when provided with equal opportunities, female leaders possess the capability to drive substantial change and introduce innovative perspectives to the business world. Her leadership has not only transformed Stitch Fix into a powerhouse of innovation and success but has also set a precedent for the role of women in leadership, inspiring future generations to break barriers and redefine the norms of industry leadership.

Beyond her business achievements, Lake has become a role model for women aiming to break the glass ceiling in tech and entrepreneurship. Her ability to challenge the status quo and drive meaningful change has motivated many women to pursue leadership positions, thereby contributing to a shift towards greater gender diversity in traditionally male-dominated fields.

Future Outlook

Katrina Lake's legacy with Stitch Fix extends far beyond the company's financial success; it signifies a monumental shift in the industry's approach to leadership and diversity. Her accomplishments resonate deeply with the statement 'the future is female,' illustrating that with vision, resilience, and innovative thinking, women can redefine the business landscape. Looking forward, Lake's influence is expected to pave the way for future generations of women leaders, further transforming tech and retail sectors to be more inclusive, dynamic, and diverse.

Lake's story shows the importance of market disruption, leadership diversity, and achieving firsts in public listings as key success metrics. These achievements not only benchmark Lake's personal success but also signal broader industry trends towards inclusivity and innovation.

By examining Katrina Lake's entrepreneurial journey and the ascent of Stitch Fix, this case study aims to inspire and empower women entrepreneurs, professional women in business, and those in the tech industry. It provides invaluable tactics to overcoming challenges, seizing opportunities, and creating a legacy that impacts both the present and the future of enterprise.

Redefining the Future with Reshma Saujani

Reshma Saujani, the visionary behind the Girls Who Code initiative, has catalyzed a paradigm shift in how female leadership, technological education, and empowerment are perceived and actualized in the 21st century. This case study outlines Saujani's key achievements, the significant impact of her work on the 'future is female' movement, success stories from those touched by her efforts, and the enduring ripple effects through technology, education, and leadership circles.

Reshma Saujani embarked on a groundbreaking mission to disrupt the traditional norms and practices, driven by a fervent passion to close the significant gender gap in technology. Her vision extended beyond just bridging this divide; she aimed to foster a new model of female leadership that is rooted deeply in the principles of bravery and the acceptance of failure as a stepping stone to success. With a dynamic and diverse background that spans across the legal, political, and social sectors, Saujani has uniquely positioned herself as a pivotal and influential figure in the realm of gender equality and technological advocacy. Her efforts are not just aimed at creating opportunities for women in technology but are also directed towards inspiring a cultural shift that embraces diversity, innovation, and resilience. Through her work, Saujani is advocating for profound change, challenging societal norms, and paving the way for future generations of women to lead with confidence and courage.

Empowering Future Coders

Founded by Reshma Saujani in 2012, Girls Who Code has rapidly evolved from a modest initiative into a transformative force within the tech industry, steadfastly dedicated to empowering young women. By equipping them with essential computing skills, it aims to close the gender gap in technology fields. Its mission is deeply rooted in inspiring these girls to confidently pursue careers in technology, a sector where women have been historically underrepresented and often overlooked.

Through a variety of well-structured initiatives, including intensive summer immersion programs, engaging after-school clubs, and supportive college loops, Girls Who Code delivers a well thought-out, impactful approach to education in technology. These programs aren't just about coding; they cover a broad spectrum of tech disciplines, including robotics, web development, and much more, providing hands-on experience and fostering a solid foundation in each area.

To date, Girls Who Code has made a remarkable impact on the landscape of technology education, reaching over 90,000 girls across all 50 states, including many from underserved and underprivileged communities. This wide-reaching influence is a testament to its success in breaking down socio-economic barriers and fostering an inclusive, supportive community. By normalizing success in technology for women and ensuring they have access to the necessary support, resources, and network, Girls Who Code is not just teaching girls to code but is reshaping the future of the tech industry to be more inclusive and diverse.

By creating a nurturing environment where young women can learn, grow, and thrive in the field of technology, Girls Who Code is laying the groundwork for a future where gender disparity in tech is a thing of the past. This visionary organization continues to inspire, motivate, and empower the next generation of female tech leaders, ensuring they are well-prepared to contribute to and excel in a rapidly evolving industry.

Key Achievements

Surpassing its initial goals by a considerable margin, Girls Who Code, a non-profit organization, has redefined the benchmarks for educating and inspiring girls in the domains of computing and technology. Through the provision of extensive resources, dedicated mentorship, and unwavering community support, Girls Who Code has not only made significant strides but has also played a pivotal role in bridging the gender gap within STEM fields. By fostering an inclusive environment that encourages learning and innovation, this organization has empowered countless girls to pursue careers in technology and computing, further contributing to a diverse and dynamic workforce.

Reshma Saujani's groundbreaking book, *Women Who Don't Wait in Line*, stands as another inspirational symbol for women across the globe. This compelling call to arms challenges the conventional narratives of success that have often limited women's aspirations. Instead, it encourages women to craft their own definitions of success, emphasizing the importance of personal fulfillment over societal expectations. By advocating for bold risk-taking and unwavering resilience, Saujani inspires women to venture beyond their comfort zones and assume leadership roles that were historically beyond reach. This influential work not only seeks to empower women to shatter the glass ceilings that have constrained them but also to carve out new paths marked by innovation, leadership, and unapologetic ambition. It's a testament to the belief that women, when they harness their unique strengths and challenge the status quo, can enact profound changes both in their personal lives and in the wider world.

In the pivotal year of 2010, she broke significant ground by becoming the first Indian American woman to run for U.S. Congress. This historic move not only showcased her pioneering spirit but also laid a solid foundation for future generations of Indian American women. Her candidacy was a shining example of hope and a strong statement in the political landscape, encouraging them to step into political arenas and make their voices heard on a national stage. Her bold step forward was not just about representation; it was about challenging the status quo and inspiring a wave of political engagement among communities that had been historically underrepresented.

Reshaping Perspectives

Saujani's exceptional efforts have been instrumental in catalyzing significant strides towards gender equality, focusing especially on dismantling the longstanding barriers within technology and leadership spheres. Her innovative philosophy champions the notion that bravery should be valued above the quest for perfection. She offers a refreshing perspective on failure, viewing it not as a hindrance but as an essential stepping stone toward success. This perspective has ignited a potent cultural and professional transformation across various industries, fostering an environment that encourages and celebrates female participation and leadership.

This transformative approach has deeply resonated within communities, sparking a movement that champions change and empowers women and girls across the nation. It has given them the courage and motivation to pursue careers in the STEM fields—science, technology, engineering, and mathematics—and to assume leadership roles with confidence. They are now more equipped than ever to navigate and overcome the traditional barriers that might have deterred their predecessors, as well as to face the fear of failure with a newfound resilience.

Saujani's work goes beyond mere advocacy; it has actively challenged and changed the prevailing perceptions around women's capabilities and rights to access and excel in areas previously dominated by men. By doing so, she has paved the way for a more inclusive and equitable environment, not just for the current generation but also for those to come. Her efforts have laid the groundwork for a future where women and girls, bolstered by the principles of courage and resilience, can aspire to and achieve their fullest potential without the constraints of outdated societal norms. This legacy of empowerment stands as a testament to Saujani's visionary impact, promising a brighter, more inclusive future for all.

Impactful Moments

A Girls Who Code alum, having graduated from the program, has successfully transitioned into a thriving computer science major at her university. This remarkable young woman directly attributes her decision to pursue a career in computer science to the transformative experience she had during a summer immersion program with Girls Who Code. This immersion wasn't just about learning to code; it was an introduction to the world of technology, providing her with valuable skills, insights, and the confidence necessary to navigate the male-dominated tech industry.

Her time spent coding and engaging with technology during those formative summer months played an absolutely pivotal role in shaping her future aspirations and career path. This experience exemplifies the profound impact that early exposure to coding and technology can have on young women, inspiring them to envision a future for themselves in the tech industry.

A dedicated educator from a rural school has recently shared an inspiring observation: there has been a significant boost in the confidence levels among female students participating in the Girls Who Code program. This remarkable increase in self-assurance among these young women is especially noteworthy. Previously hesitant and reserved, many of these students are now ambitiously considering futures in the fields of Science, Technology, Engineering, and Mathematics (STEM)—sectors that have historically been male-dominated.

This transformation is not just a testament to the empowering effect of the program but also an encouraging indicator of shifting perspectives towards gender diversity in STEM professions. The educator's observation supports the vital role that educational initiatives can play in opening up new horizons for students, challenging traditional stereotypes, and fostering a more inclusive environment in areas of study and work that have long been in need of diversity.

After immersing in the captivating narrative of *Women Who Don't Wait in Line*, an impressive number of readers have come forward to express how this book has profoundly influenced their lives. They share personal tales of transformation, deeply inspired by Reshma Saujani's insightful observations and motivational guidance, which have acted as a spark for significant personal growth. These individuals recount the challenges they faced, including overcoming formidable barriers and challenging deep-rooted societal expectations.

They were motivated by the empowering message of the book, which inspired them not just to dream of leadership roles but to actively pursue and attain them, despite facing and overcoming numerous obstacles along the way. The shared stories define the book's remarkable ability to inspire change, encouraging readers to chase their dreams with unwavering determination and resilience. This clear message of empowerment extends beyond the pages, fostering a community of individuals who are inspired to break molds, challenge the status quo, and redefine their paths to success, all while supporting each other in their journeys of personal and professional growth.

> *"Teach Girls Bravery, Not Perfection."*
> —Reshma Saujani

This rallying cry by Saujani has not only become synonymous with the Girls Who Code movement but also serves as a foundational principle for rethinking female empowerment in the digital age. It brings to the surface the necessity of building a society where young women are encouraged to be bold, take risks, and lean into the discomfort of uncertainty.

The trajectory of Reshma Saujani's work extends beyond the tangible metrics of success. It lies in the vibrancy of a community unafraid to fail, to try again, and to dream bigger. Her unwavering commitment to transforming the landscape for young women in technology and leadership continues to inspire and mobilize action. As we look toward the future, Saujani's vision for a more inclusive and equitable world serves as a guiding light, celebrating the next generation of female leaders and innovators.

The implications of Saujani's work for gender equality and empowerment are far-reaching. In a world where the technological divide is narrowing, her efforts ensure that women are not only participants but leaders in shaping the future. For all tech industry leaders, women in tech, and women entrepreneurs considering a tech-based business model, the story of Reshma Saujani is a testament to the impact one individual can have on the whole of society, urging us all to envision and strive for a world where the future truly is female.

Anne Wojcicki and 23andMe

Anne Wojcicki, co-founder and CEO of 23andMe, has emerged as a formidable force in the biotechnology and health industry. Under her leadership, 23andMe has transcended the boundaries of traditional healthcare and genetic research, empowering individuals to access and understand their genetic makeup. This case study explores Wojcicki's key achievements, the impact of her work, and the distinctive qualities that set 23andMe apart from its competitors.

Pioneering Personal Genomics

Launched in 2006, 23andMe completely shattered the traditional
mold of genetic testing, a field that was previously confined to
the exclusive realms of medical practitioners and researchers. It
introduced a groundbreaking direct-to-consumer genetic testing
service, marking a pivotal shift in the accessibility of genetic
information. This revolutionary approach granted individuals
unprecedented insight into their personal ancestry, potential
health predispositions, and a myriad of genetic traits. By doing so,
it effectively democratized access to genetic information, making
it accessible to the general public for the first time.

Anne Wojcicki, the visionary behind 23andMe, had a clear and
compelling vision: to profoundly enhance our understanding
of human genetics in a manner that fosters proactive health
management. She envisioned a world where individuals are
empowered with knowledge about their own bodies, enabling
them to make informed decisions about their health and wellness.
This vision was not just about providing access to genetic
information but about sparking a transformation in the way
people think about their health, genetics, and the potential for
future medical breakthroughs.

By empowering individuals with this level of insight into their
genetics, 23andMe has not only revolutionized the way we think
about genetics and health but has also ignited a global conversation
on the ethical, legal, and social implications of easy access to

genetic information. The company's impact extends beyond individual health management, influencing research, policy, and societal understanding of genetics. It challenges us to consider the ramifications of genetic knowledge—how it can be used, who has access to it, and how it shapes our understanding of identity, family, and race.

In essence, 23andMe's innovative approach has paved the way for a new era in genetic understanding, making it an instrumental force in the ongoing exploration of the human genome. Its contributions continue to influence the fields of medicine, genetics, and even sociology, marking a significant milestone in the journey toward a more informed and health-conscious society.

Her Impact on Healthcare

23andMe has been a groundbreaking force in transforming how individuals engage with their health and genetic information. It has fostered a paradigm shift towards a more informed and proactive approach in managing personal health. By making personal genomics accessible to a broad audience, 23andMe has not just democratized access to crucial genetic information but has also played a significant role in shaping health policy and advancing advocacy for patient rights across the globe.

Its meticulous services provide important statistics into one's genetic predispositions and potential health risks, thereby fostering a greater public understanding of genetics. This enhanced understanding has, in turn, paved the way for more informed healthcare decisions. Individuals are now better equipped to engage in meaningful conversations with their healthcare providers, making choices that are tailored to their unique genetic makeup. This shift unveils the critical importance of having individual access to one's own health data.

The contributions of 23andMe have ignited a wide-ranging conversation about the ethical, social, and legal implications of genetic testing. This ongoing dialogue has encouraged continuous research and debate in the field, bringing to light various perspectives on privacy, consent, and the potential for genetic discrimination. It has sparked a vital discussion on how to responsibly harness the power of genomics in healthcare while safeguarding individual rights and privacy.

Through its innovative approach, 23andMe has exemplified the transformative potential of personal genomics in revolutionizing healthcare and personalized medicine. By providing individuals with unprecedented access to their genetic information, it empowers them to take charge of their health in ways that were previously unimaginable. As a result, 23andMe stands as an instrumental force in shaping the future of health management, illustrating the profound impact that accessible genetic information can have on society at large.

Driving Research Collaborations

One of Anne Wojcicki's most remarkable achievements is her unparalleled success in establishing research collaborations with premier organizations within the pharmaceutical and biotech sectors, a feat not easily accomplished in such competitive industries. These strategic partnerships have not only been beneficial for both parties involved but have played a pivotal role in hastening the advent of innovative treatments and cures that leverage profound genetic insights. This careful orchestration of collaborations positions 23andMe's vital contribution beyond its initial offering of genetic testing services and showcases its role as a catalyst in the ever-evolving healthcare landscape.

These partnerships boost 23andMe's influential position in shaping the trajectory of personalized medicine and drug development, areas that promise to revolutionize how diseases are treated. By effectively bridging the gap between vast genetic data and therapeutic application, Wojcicki has masterfully positioned 23andMe at the forefront of a healthcare revolution. In this new era, customized treatment plans based on individual genetic profiles are becoming the norm, thereby transforming patient care for the better. This transformation speaks volumes about the potential of personalized medicine to not only enhance the efficacy of treatments but also to dramatically improve patient outcomes by tailoring healthcare to the unique genetic makeup of each individual.

Anne Wojcicki's visionary leadership and strategic foresight have therefore not only propelled 23andMe to success but have also paved the way for a future where healthcare is more personalized, effective, and patient-centric. Through her efforts, Wojcicki has not just advanced the field of genetic testing but has also contributed significantly to the broader realm of medicine, setting a new standard for how companies can contribute to the advancement of healthcare and treatment methodologies.

Advocacy and Recognition

Wojcicki's relentless and tireless advocacy for healthcare reform, complemented by her unwavering commitment to individual empowerment, serves as a robust testament to her dedication toward the radical transformation of the healthcare industry. Globally recognized as one of the most influential and powerful women in technology, Wojcicki's pioneering efforts have steadfastly focused on democratizing access to health information. With a passionate belief in the strength of empowering individuals, she argues that giving people the ability to access their own health data is not just a luxury but a fundamental necessity. This, she firmly believes, is crucial for enabling more informed decision-making and significantly enhancing the quality of patient care overall.

Wojcicki's vision extends far beyond mere access to information; it encompasses a holistic approach towards health literacy, encouraging a profound understanding of personal health metrics and their implications on one's wellbeing. This philosophy is at the heart of 23andMe, the company she leads masterfully, which has been instrumental in revolutionizing how individuals engage with their health data. The company's services, which enable users to gain information into their genetic predispositions and health risks through simple tests, are a significant leap forward in making healthcare more accessible and understandable to the general public.

The impact of Wojcicki's work is reflected not only in the countless testimonials from thoroughly satisfied customers but also in the highly positive feedback from respected health industry experts. These testimonials and expert endorsements significantly demonstrate the transformative and groundbreaking impact of her work. They widely praise 23andMe for its innovative approach in reintroducing a much-needed human element back into the often impersonal and complex healthcare system. By doing so, it marks a notable shift towards more personalized and compassionate healthcare solutions. This approach has not only changed how individuals perceive their health but has also started a broader conversation on the importance of personalized healthcare in improving patient outcomes and satisfaction.

In essence, Wojcicki's contributions to the healthcare field extend well beyond the scope of her company. Her advocacy for healthcare reform, combined with a deep-seated belief in the importance of individual empowerment, has set a new benchmark in the industry. It paves the way for a future where healthcare is more personalized, accessible, and, most importantly, centered around the unique needs and circumstances of each individual.

Competitive Edge

23andMe distinguishes itself in the competitive market with its extensive personal genomics service, offering an unparalleled, robust, and user-friendly platform that truly stands out from the rest. This pioneering company is deeply committed to consumer privacy, demonstrating an unwavering dedication to the protection and security of user data, a concern that is paramount in today's digital age. Moreover, 23andMe doesn't just rest on its laurels; through strategic research collaborations with leading institutions and innovative companies, it continuously enhances its offerings. These partnerships enable 23andMe to provide cutting-edge and deeply useful medical information to consumers, further enriching its service portfolio.

Unlike its competitors, 23andMe offers a thorough one-stop-shop for genetic information. This extensive service includes detailed ancestry reports that trace back your lineage, health risk assessments that prepare you for future medical possibilities, and traits analysis that uncovers the genetic basis of various personal characteristics. By delivering a holistic view of one's genetic makeup, 23andMe stands as a leader in the field, providing x-ray vision into both where we come from and what might lie ahead in our health futures.

All of this is achieved with a steadfast commitment to prioritizing top-notch data security, adhering to the highest ethical practices in every facet of their operations. In a world increasingly concerned with data privacy, 23andMe's rigorous standards set a benchmark for what consumer data protection should look like.

At the helm of 23andMe is Anne Wojcicki, whose visionary leadership and relentless pursuit of innovation have been instrumental in the company's ascent to become a trusted name in the realm of personal genomics. Her foresight and dedication to bridging the gap between complex genetic information and actionable health solutions have not only propelled 23andMe forward but have also significantly advanced the field of genomics. Under her guidance, 23andMe doesn't merely offer a glimpse into genetic predispositions; it empowers individuals with knowledge to make informed health and lifestyle decisions. This empowerment plays a pivotal role in the future of personalized healthcare and wellness, marking 23andMe as not just a company, but a movement towards a more informed, health-conscious society.

23andMe, through its innovative platform, commitment to privacy and security, along with its leadership in the personal genomics space, is paving the way for a new era of personalized healthcare. By empowering individuals with detailed comprehension of their genetic makeup, 23andMe is not only enhancing the way people understand their ancestry and health risks but is also contributing significantly to the broader field of genomics and personalized medicine.

Future Outlook

Looking ahead, 23andMe is poised to continue its role as a trailblazer in the rapidly expanding field of personal genomics. Despite navigating through a complex landscape filled with formidable regulatory hurdles and the relentless pace of technological innovation, the company's unwavering dedication to groundbreaking research, combined with its stringent privacy protocols, sets it apart. Its mission to empower individuals with knowledge about their own genetics places it squarely at the forefront of the dynamic and evolving dialogue surrounding personalized healthcare and genomics.

This commitment not only positions 23andMe as a key player in the industry but also as a visionary leader shaping the future of how we understand and approach our health and well-being through the advanced lens of genomics. By harnessing the power of genetic information, 23andMe aims to revolutionize our approach to healthcare, making personalized health strategies more accessible and applicable to the everyday lives of people around the globe. This vision of personalized healthcare, underpinned by the latest advancements in genomics, promises to transform our approach to disease prevention, diagnosis, and treatment, making 23andMe a critical force in the journey towards more individualized health solutions.

Anne Wojcicki's exemplary leadership and forward-thinking vision have adeptly navigated the company 23andMe through the uncharted territories of the burgeoning field of personal genomics and healthcare. By transforming the landscape of how individuals access and understand their genetic information, Wojcicki has played a critical role in shaping the future of personalized medicine. With a relentless commitment to empowering individuals with access to their own genetic data, she has also driven significant research collaborations that have the potential to unearth groundbreaking medical discoveries.

Her unwavering commitment to healthcare reform has established her as a powerful catalyst for change in an industry often resistant to transformation. Under her guidance, 23andMe has not only provided millions of people with invaluable facts of their health and ancestry but has also sparked a global conversation about the importance of genetic privacy and ethical data use.

Wojcicki's achievements underline the profound and lasting impact of 23andMe on individual health management and the broader health ecosystem, cementing her legacy as a true pioneer and innovator in the industry.

Sara Blakely's Spanx Empire

Sara Blakely, the visionary behind the Spanx brand, has not only revolutionized the shapewear industry but has also established herself as a steward of innovation, resilience, and philanthropy in the business world. This case study aims to dissect the key achievements of Blakely's entrepreneurial journey, her profound impact on women in business and entrepreneurship, and the unique process that set her apart as a role model for future generations.

In a world where female entrepreneurs are steadily carving their niche, Sara Blakely stands out as a pioneer. Her creation, Spanx, has become a household name, offering a wide range of undergarments that prioritize both comfort and aesthetics. Beyond her commercial success, Blakely's decision to sign the Giving Pledge and her continuous efforts to empower women globally through various initiatives have cemented her position as one of the most influential women in the world.

Early Life and Career

Blakely's journey to the pinnacle of entrepreneurial success was a winding path, filled with numerous challenges and obstacles that would have deterred a less determined individual. The early rejections from investors and the professional setbacks she encountered along her journey did not deter her; instead, they fueled her determination to succeed against the odds. It was during her late 20s, after years of experiencing discomfort and dissatisfaction with the available shapewear options, that Blakely conceived the innovative idea of creating comfortable, effective, and aesthetically pleasing shapewear that would meet the needs of women everywhere.

This revolutionary idea laid the groundwork for what would eventually become Spanx, a brand that turned the shapewear industry on its head. Blakely's story is not just one of achieving business success; it is a powerful testament to the power of resilience, innovative thinking, and an unwavering commitment to pursuing one's dreams, no matter how insurmountable the challenges may seem. Through her journey, Blakely has inspired countless aspiring entrepreneurs to persevere, innovate, and remain committed to their vision.

Founding of Spanx

The inception of Spanx by Sara Blakely completely revolutionized the shapewear industry, marking an unprecedented turning point in how women approached their wardrobes across the globe. Sara Blakely's direct, innovative approach to directly addressing women's needs through functional, comfortable, and immensely flattering undergarments filled a significant and previously unnoticed gap in the market. This gap, one that many weren't even aware existed until Spanx came along, brought forth how traditional shapewear was failing to meet the modern woman's desire for both comfort and style.

Sara Blakely's products were not just garments; they were confidence boosters that addressed common wardrobe malfunctions and challenges, empowering countless women worldwide to feel better about their appearance and, by extension, themselves. The unique selling proposition of Spanx lay not only in its functionality but in how it made women feel: more confident, poised, and self-assured.

However, Blakely's journey to success was not a smooth path. She faced considerable challenges, especially in the early days when she sought to bring her innovative vision to life. Despite facing initial skepticism and resistance from manufacturers who failed to see the potential in her ideas, her unwavering belief in her product's value and her relentless pursuit of excellence were instrumental in overcoming these hurdles. This part of the Spanx story powerfully showcases the importance of persistence and resilience in entrepreneurship, especially for women venturing into predominantly male industries.

Sara Blakely's ability to tirelessly push for the realization of her vision, overcoming obstacle after obstacle with grace and determination, is a testament to the impact one individual can have on an industry through sheer determination and an unwavering belief in their idea. She not only transformed the shapewear industry but also set a new standard for women's undergarments, pioneering a space where function and fashion coexist harmoniously.

Her story is an inspirational reminder for aspiring entrepreneurs that with hard work, innovative thinking, and a never-give-up attitude, transforming an industry and making a lasting contribution is entirely possible. It supports the power of a single visionary to effect change and inspire others to pursue their dreams with the same fervor and resilience. Sara Blakely's Spanx empire stands as a testament of success to anyone looking to make their mark in their field, proving that with passion, determination, and a solution-oriented approach, achieving groundbreaking success is within reach.

Financial Milestones

Spanx, with its valuation now impressively surpassing the one billion mark, has positioned its founder, Sara Blakely, as the youngest self-made female billionaire, a title that dramatically changes the financial success and widespread global impact of her brand. This significant achievement not only encompasses Blakely's entrepreneurial spirit but also showcases her exceptional ability to identify and tap into a market need with innovative solutions that resonate deeply with consumers. Spanx's product line, known for its innovation and quality, is extensively available across more than 50 countries, amplifying the universal appeal and demand for Blakely's innovations. This wide distribution network showcases how the brand has resonated with consumers worldwide, irrespective of cultural and geographical boundaries.

The global footprint of Spanx is not just a testament to the brand's versatility and quality, but it also reflects its founder's visionary approach to empowering women by making them feel confident and comfortable in their own skin. Blakely's journey from the initial concept to creating a globally recognized brand speaks volumes of her determination, creativity, and understanding of women's needs. The brand's success is further amplified by its commitment to innovation and quality, ensuring that each product not only meets but exceeds consumer expectations. This holistic vision and relentless pursuit of excellence have not only carved a niche for Spanx in the competitive market but have also set a new standard for what is possible in the industry, inspiring aspiring entrepreneurs worldwide.

Philanthropy and Women Empowerment

The Sara Blakely Foundation, founded by the entrepreneurial powerhouse behind Spanx, Sara Blakely, stands as a monumental testament to Blakely's undeniable commitment to philanthropy. This foundation has made a remarkable impact by positively affecting the lives of over 200,000 women across the globe through its strategic entrepreneurial training and support programs. These initiatives, meticulously designed by Blakely and her team, are crafted not only to foster growth and empowerment among women but also to instill a sense of confidence and independence.

The foundation's approach to philanthropy is multifaceted, generously providing scholarships to aspiring female entrepreneurs, mentorship opportunities with seasoned business leaders, and a plethora of resources tailored to meet the unique challenges faced by women in the business world. The goal is clear: to elevate the role of women in the business realm and to ensure that they have a significant, lasting impact.

Testimonials from the beneficiaries of these programs demonstrate the profound and tangible impact of Blakely's efforts. These stories of transformation and success serve as the guiding light and inspiration to women worldwide, illustrating the powerful ripple effect of empowerment. They not only reflect the immediate benefits of such support—such as launching successful businesses, achieving financial independence, and gaining leadership skills—but also illustrate the long-term empowerment and increased opportunities these women experience.

These success stories, shared through various platforms and speaking engagements, have inspired a broader conversation about the role of women in entrepreneurship and the importance of supporting female-led businesses. This dialogue has encouraged more organizations to invest in women, proving the enduring value of Blakely's vision in empowering women across the globe.

The Sara Blakely Foundation is more than a charitable entity; it is a lighthouse of hope and a catalyst for change, dedicated to breaking barriers and forging a path for women's success in the business world and beyond. Through its framework of programs and unwavering support, the foundation not only empowers women to achieve their dreams but also contributes to a more inclusive and equitable business landscape.

Recognition and Influence

Blakely's prestigious recognition by TIME Magazine as one
of the most influential people in the world stands as a
powerful testament to her extraordinary contributions to the
global business landscape. This honor key points not just her
business acumen but also acknowledges her exceptional leadership
skills, which, when combined with her significant philanthropic
endeavors, have set a remarkably high bar in the industry. Her
efforts have not only reshaped the way female entrepreneurship is
viewed but continue to inspire countless women across the globe
to passionately pursue their entrepreneurial dreams.

By boldly challenging traditional norms and breaking barriers in
the realms of business and entrepreneurship, Blakely has paved the
way for future generations of women to succeed in areas that were
previously dominated by men. Her relentless pursuit of gender
equality in the business world has made her an iconic figure and
a hero for many. Her innovative approach to leadership and her
commitment to making a difference in the world through her
philanthropic efforts further solidify her status as a role model.

In doing so, Blakely has contributed significantly to the movement
towards gender equality in the business world. Her legacy includes
not only the success of her own endeavors but also the doors
she has opened for women who dream of achieving similar
heights in their respective fields. Through her actions, Blakely has
demonstrated that with determination, courage, and a willingness

to challenge the status quo, it is possible to make a lasting impact on the world.

Uniqueness and Future Outlook

Sara's entrepreneurial philosophy, emphasizing perseverance, innovation, and philanthropy, offers invaluable examples for aspiring entrepreneurs. Her story exemplifies how turning personal challenges into opportunities can lead to groundbreaking success. Looking ahead, Spanx's trajectory under Blakely's leadership, alongside her philanthropic initiatives, promises continued innovation and impact on global entrepreneurship and women's empowerment.

Sara Blakely's legacy transcends the confines of the apparel industry, embodying the essence of entrepreneurial spirit, resilience, grit, and true philanthropy.

No Permission Needed

"The question isn't who's going to let me; it's who is going to stop me."

—Ayn Rand

This quote encapsulates the spirit of this chapter. Women in business today are not waiting for permission; we are carving our paths, driven by determination and a resolute willingness to dream big. To women aspiring to make their mark in the business world, the message is clear—the future is not just female; the future is ours for the taking.

This chapter was designed to inspire, inform, and *energize* you. My goal is to offer women in business—and all readers—a meaningful perspective on the transformative progress being made toward gender equality. As we continue to push for progress and greater representation of women in the business world, it is important to acknowledge and celebrate the strides that have already been made. From breaking glass ceilings to closing the gender pay gap, women have proven time and time again our ability to excel in all industries.

May these observations serve as our roadmap, guiding future entrepreneurs and leaders towards a more inclusive, innovative, and equitable business world for all of us.

Key Takeaways and Concluding Thoughts

One crucial key takeaway from this article is the importance of representation. Seeing successful women in leadership positions can inspire others to pursue their own entrepreneurial dreams. It is also crucial for companies to prioritize diversity and inclusion initiatives, as research shows that diverse teams lead to better decision-making and overall success.

The power of mentorship is another crucial key. As we strive for gender equality in the business world, it is important for established professionals to offer guidance and support to up-and-coming female leaders. Mentorship programs can provide valuable resources, advice, and connections for aspiring entrepreneurs.

Mentorship, access to funding and resources is crucial for women pursuing entrepreneurial endeavors. While there are still disparities in funding opportunities for women-owned businesses, there has been a rise in initiatives aimed at supporting female entrepreneurs. These include organizations that provide grants, loans, and educational resources specifically tailored to the needs of women entrepreneurs.

Companies can also play a role in promoting gender equality by implementing policies that support work-life balance and offer equal opportunities for advancement. This not only benefits individual employees but also leads to a more inclusive and productive workplace culture.

Ultimately, seeing representation and having access to necessary resources are key factors in empowering women to pursue their entrepreneurial dreams.

Reflective Questions For You, the Reader

- What steps can companies take to promote gender

equality and create a more inclusive and balanced workplace?

- How can your workplace support women entrepreneurs in their journey?

- What, if any, financial barriers have you faced as an inspiring entrepreneur and how have you overcome them?

- How can we continue to challenge and break gender stereotypes in the workplace?

- What actions can individuals take to support gender equality in their daily lives and interactions with others?

6

Branding With Purpose

I n today's highly competitive marketplace, brands that stand
for something beyond profits are the ones that capture
hearts and minds. In this chapter, we discuss the profound
impact of values in branding, showcasing real-world examples
of companies that have built their identities around purpose
and social responsibility. These brands don't just tell a story;
they embody their beliefs through every facet of their business
operations, forging deeper connections with consumers and
setting new standards in their industries.

With consumers increasingly seeking authenticity and meaning
in their purchases, the concept of branding with purpose has
never been more crucial. This chapter will guide you through
the significance of integrating core values and social responsibility
into your brand strategy, illustrating how doing so can enhance
consumer perception, foster loyalty, and drive sustainable growth.

The Role of Values in Brand Identity and Business Operations

Values serve as the critical foundational pillar of any brand's identity, profoundly shaping the manner in which businesses conduct themselves both internally and in their engagement with the wider world. Let's discuss the remarkable impact that values hold over every aspect of a company's operations. From the nurturing of a unique internal culture that resonates with employees to the strategic carving of a distinctive niche within the competitive marketplace, values are instrumental.

Through detailed examination of examples from globally renowned brands such as Patagonia, TOMS, Ben & Jerry's, and Dove, this analysis will explain how these entities' unwavering dedication to their core values has not merely influenced their strategic business moves but has fundamentally shaped their communication with customers. Each of these brands has demonstrated a strong commitment to their values, guiding them through challenges and informing their strategies and marketing efforts.

Patagonia's environmental activism, TOMS' shoe donation program, Ben & Jerry's commitment to social justice, and Dove's promotion of body positivity illustrate how deeply a brand's values can resonate with consumers, differentiating these brands in highly competitive markets. Their dedication to their core values fosters a strong, emotional connection with target audiences, encouraging customer loyalty that transcends the ordinary, leading to lasting customer loyalty.

By analyzing how these brands seamlessly integrate their values into both their operational practices and their messaging, we can gain valuable comprehension into the critical importance of these values in constructing a resilient and distinctive brand identity. It becomes clear that values are not just abstract principles; they are actionable guideposts that inform every decision and interaction, helping to build a brand that stands the test of time in a fluctuating market landscape.

Examples of Purpose-Driven Branding Done Right

Patagonia's Trailblazing environmental activism

From their groundbreaking advertising campaigns to their commitment to sustainable materials and production practices, Patagonia's dedication to environmental activism has been integral to their brand identity since day one. By aligning with like-minded organizations and leveraging their platform for social change, the company has established itself as a leader in purpose-driven branding. The company distinguishes itself not only through its superior outdoor equipment but also as a shining example of environmental and social responsibility. Established with a deep-seated commitment to the welfare of the planet, this ethos is embedded in Patagonia's DNA, influencing every decision and action the company takes. Its dedication is evident in the meticulous selection of sustainable materials, efforts to reduce carbon footprint, and initiatives aimed at preserving natural habitats. By putting its core values of environmental protection and social responsibility at the forefront of its business strategy, Patagonia has become a leading force in corporate sustainability efforts, inspiring others in the industry to follow suit.

Key Environmental Initiatives

Patagonia's holistic approach to environmental activism encompasses a wide range of strategies that go beyond the mere creation of eco-friendly products. This approach includes a bold consideration of the product life cycle, operational impacts, community engagement, and broader global conservation efforts. Patagonia's initiatives are not only ambitious but also serve as a model for corporate responsibility in environmental stewardship. Here are some of the key initiatives that reflect Patagonia's commitment:

Worn Wear Program

More than just a campaign, the Worn Wear Program embodies an innovative movement towards sustainability. It encourages customers to repair, reuse, and recycle their clothing, which not only reduces waste but also challenges the prevailing culture of consumerism. By promoting sustainable consumption, Patagonia is leading the charge in shifting consumer behavior towards more environmentally friendly practices. Patagonia's innovative Worn Wear Program has successfully kept thousands of tons of textiles from ending up in landfills, showcasing the program's remarkable effectiveness in promoting waste reduction. This initiative not only encourages recycling and reuse but also challenges the culture of fast fashion by extending the life of clothing.

1% For the Planet

Demonstrating a profound commitment to the environment, Patagonia pledges 1% of its total sales to environmental nonprofits, a move that has funneled significant financial resources into conservation and sustainability projects across the globe. This initiative not only provides essential funding for environmental efforts but also sets a precedent for corporate giving, inspiring other companies to contribute towards the planet's well-being.

Patagonia Action Works

In an effort to bridge the gap between individuals and environmental causes, the company launched Patagonia Action Works. By empowering grassroots activism, Patagonia is helping to create a network of engaged citizens committed to environmental protection and conservation. The Patagonia Action Works platform has been a catalyst for change, with tens of thousands of volunteer hours logged. This engagement has led to notable

conservation achievements and has played a crucial role in
enriching communities by connecting individuals with local
environmental actions.

Renewable Energy Transition

In a bold move towards sustainability, Patagonia has transitioned
to using 100% renewable energy sources in all its stores, offices,
and distribution centers. This significant shift not only reduces the
company's carbon footprint but also serves as a powerful statement
on the feasibility and importance of renewable energy. Through
this initiative, Patagonia is leading by example, showing the world
that sustainable operations are not only possible but also practical.
Patagonia's shift towards renewable energy sources has led to a
measurable reduction in greenhouse gas emissions. This successful
transition powers the company's dedication to sustainability and
its role as a leader in the fight against climate change.

Sustainable Sourcing Practices

Patagonia's commitment to environmental activism extends
into its sourcing practices. By choosing organic cotton and
recycled materials, Patagonia is setting new industry standards
for sustainability. This dedication to sustainable sourcing not
only minimizes environmental impact but also influences other
companies to adopt more eco-friendly practices. Through these
efforts, Patagonia is driving a revolution in sustainable sourcing,
proving that responsible production is within reach for the

entire industry. These initiatives collectively embody Patagonia's pioneering spirit and its unwavering commitment to protecting the planet. By addressing environmental issues on multiple fronts, Patagonia is not just making a statement; it's paving the way for a more sustainable future. In a commendable effort to reduce its environmental footprint, over 75% of all Patagonia products are now made with recycled materials. This significant achievement brings to the forefront the company's commitment to sustainable sourcing practices and sets a benchmark for the industry in minimizing environmental impact.

Challenges and Solutions

Implementing these initiatives wasn't without its hurdles. From sourcing challenges, such as finding sustainable materials that met their strict environmental standards, to engaging the community, which involved educating and rallying support around their environmental mission, Patagonia faced numerous obstacles. However, the company addressed these challenges through innovation, by developing new, eco-friendly materials; perseverance, by continuously pushing forward despite setbacks; and a steadfast commitment to its values, never wavering in its mission to save our planet. This approach not only helped overcome the obstacles but also strengthened Patagonia's leadership in environmental advocacy.

Broader Implications

Patagonia's unwavering commitment to environmental activism
has substantially influenced not only its own industry but also
the broader scope of society. This renowned outdoor brand
has boldly prioritized the health of our planet over the pursuit
of profits, fundamentally redefining the essence of corporate
responsibility. By integrating sustainability into the core of
their business model, Patagonia has established new standards
for corporate behavior, serving as a symbol of inspiration for
companies worldwide. This proactive approach has encouraged
and motivated other businesses to embark on their sustainability
journeys, taking concrete actions to minimize their environmental
footprint. Patagonia's efforts vividly illustrate the influential role
that businesses can play in tackling environmental challenges,
proving that corporate entities hold significant power in steering
global efforts towards a more sustainable future. Through their
initiatives, such as funding grassroots environmental groups,
embracing fair trade practices, and consistently advocating for
the protection of untouched wild spaces, Patagonia has not
only talked the talk but walked the walk, leading by example
and showing the world that profitability and environmental
stewardship can go hand in hand.

Their steadfast dedication to environmental stewardship
has significantly elevated their brand reputation, clearly
demonstrating the substantial benefits that arise from embedding

sustainable practices into every aspect of a business. This commitment extends beyond the expected corporate social responsibility; it involves making sustainability a core principle of its business model, from product design to supply chain management. By doing so, Patagonia serves as a compelling example for other companies, showing that it's not only possible to thrive financially by prioritizing the planet but also to lead the way in positive environmental impact. This approach proves that businesses have a critical role to play in addressing global environmental challenges.

Key Takeaways and Concluding Thoughts

Patagonia's story is a powerful example of integrating environmental values into business strategy. By prioritizing sustainability, setting measurable goals, and engaging communities, Patagonia demonstrates how companies can successfully merge business success with environmental activism. Their purpose-driven approach shows the importance of corporate responsibility in addressing environmental challenges, building strong consumer connections, and operating ethically in today's world.

Reflective Questions For You, the Reader

- Does Patagonia's purpose-driven strategy inspire you to support their brand? Why or why not?

- Have you ever consciously chosen to buy from a purpose-driven brand over a competitor? If so, what motivated your decision?

- How important do you think it is for businesses to have a clear purpose and set of values? Do you believe this can impact consumer behavior and loyalty?

- In today's society, consumers are becoming increasingly conscious about the environmental and social impacts of their purchases. How do you think purpose-driven branding can help address these concerns and drive positive change in the world?

The Impact of TOMS' One for One Program

In an era where conscious consumerism is not just valued but expected, TOMS Shoes has emerged as a paragon of how companies can marry profit with purpose. At the heart of TOMS' success and its powerful appeal to consumers worldwide is its groundbreaking One for One program. This initiative encapsulates a simple yet profoundly impactful idea: for every product sold, TOMS helps a person in need. The program's reach, spanning from providing shoes and eyewear to facilitating access to clean water and supporting local economies, demonstrates the multi-dimensional impact of TOMS' commitment to making the world a better place.

Shoes for a Better Tomorrow

TOMS has made a monumental contribution by distributing over 95 million pairs of shoes to children in need around the world. This initiative goes beyond merely providing footwear; it plays a critical role in safeguarding children from soil-transmitted diseases, which are prevalent in many developing regions. By protecting children's feet, TOMS helps reduce the incidence of these diseases, contributing to the overall health and well-being of vulnerable communities. The provision of shoes also facilitates higher school attendance rates. Many children in impoverished areas are unable to attend school simply because they lack the basic necessity of shoes, which are often required for school entry. TOMS addresses this barrier by ensuring that children have proper footwear, thereby opening the door to education and the opportunities it brings. The selection process for regions where shoes are distributed is carried out with great care, focusing on areas where these contributions can have the most significant health and educational impacts. By targeting their efforts, TOMS ensures that each pair of shoes delivered maximizes the potential for positive change in the recipient's life and community.

Vision for the Future

Every purchase of eyewear results in substantial benefits for those grappling with visual impairments. From funding sight-saving surgeries that restore vision to providing prescription glasses that transform daily life, TOMS' eyewear program has made a profound impact, touching the lives of over 780,000 individuals across the globe. By not only donating eyewear but also training local health workers, the program ensures that communities receive the skilled care they need. By placing a strong emphasis on eye health education, it lays the foundation for sustainable eye care solutions, aiming to create a world where everyone has access to the eye care they deserve. This community-first approach demonstrates a deep commitment to improving vision health and quality of life for those in need, making every pair of TOMS eyewear sold a message of hope and a step towards a brighter future.

Sustainable Water Resources

The TOMS Roasting Co. initiative is an exemplary model that magnificently enhances the ecosystem of charitable giving. By committing to provide clean water to a person in need for every bag of coffee purchased, TOMS has taken a significant step towards addressing the global water crisis. This effort goes beyond mere charity; it contributes substantially to the development of sustainable water resources. By ensuring that communities have access to clean water, TOMS helps to unlock numerous health, educational, and economic benefits. Clean water means less time spent on water collection and more on productive activities, improved health due to reduced waterborne diseases, and better opportunities for education, especially for girls who often bear the burden of collecting water. This initiative demonstrates how businesses can play a vital role in solving global challenges by integrating giving into their business models.

Boosting Local Economies

An aspect of TOMS' One for One program that often goes under-appreciated is its profound positive influence on local economies where it operates. Beyond just donating shoes, TOMS actively supports jobs and encourages business growth, thereby helping to create a more robust economic environment in the communities it serves. This initiative is not just about providing immediate aid through charity; it's about empowering communities to sustain themselves and thrive long-term. By investing in local economies, TOMS is taking a holistic approach to corporate social responsibility, demonstrating that giving back can yield a wide array of benefits across various sectors. This model provides immediate relief by addressing the immediate need for shoes but also works towards building a foundation for long-term economic development and prosperity. It does so by supporting local artisans and manufacturers, which in turn stimulates local job creation and business opportunities. By encouraging the growth of local businesses, TOMS helps foster a sense of community pride and achievement, which is crucial for sustainable development. The One for One program serves as a powerful example of how socially responsible business practices can be transformative, not just for individual recipients of aid but for entire communities. It showcases the ripple effect that thoughtful, community-centric corporate policies can have, potentially inspiring other businesses to adopt similar approaches. In essence, TOMS' commitment to integrating charitable giving with support for economic development practices demands a forward-thinking approach to corporate social responsibility. This strategy exemplifies how businesses can play a crucial role in addressing global challenges, proving that corporate success and societal progress can go hand in hand.

Market Positioning and Customer Loyalty

In today's crowded marketplace, TOMS sets itself apart as the master of social responsibility. The pioneering One for One program, where every purchase supports a person in need, has been instrumental in establishing TOMS as more than just a brand; it's a movement towards global betterment. This deep-seated commitment to making a difference on a global scale resonates strongly with consumers who are increasingly conscious of their impact on the world. As a result, TOMS enjoys enhanced customer loyalty, as consumers are not just buying a product but becoming part of a larger mission to improve lives. This fosters a unique and enduring relationship between the brand and its customers, one that is built on shared values and mutual respect. By offering a purchasing experience that directly contributes to positive change, TOMS crafts a compelling brand narrative that transcends the usual transactional relationships companies have with their customers. This narrative is powerful, inspiring customers to not only embrace the brand but to become advocates for its mission. In doing so, TOMS has created a distinct position for itself in the market, one that appeals to a growing demographic of consumers who are looking to make meaningful purchases that reflect their values and aspirations for a better world. Through its innovative business model and commitment to social responsibility, TOMS not only sells products but also sells the idea of a better future, making it a true leader in the business of change.

Success Stories

Among the sea of testimonials and heartwarming success stories emanating from the One for One program initiated by TOMS, several deeply impactful narratives stand out, illuminating the profound difference this initiative makes in the lives of individuals and communities across the globe:TOMS' One for One program goes beyond traditional corporate philanthropy, embodying a deeper commitment to social responsibility that deeply intertwines with the brand's core identity. This initiative sets a precedent and raises the standards for other companies, challenging them to also prioritize social impact alongside profitability. By donating a pair of shoes for every pair sold, providing a pair of glasses for each pair purchased, and offering support through coffee sales, TOMS revolutionizes how businesses can operate with a dual focus on profit and positive social impact. The company's innovative approach showcases the potential to cultivate a successful brand that not only thrives in the marketplace but also contributes meaningfully to global communities, demonstrating that it is entirely feasible to change lives around the world—one pair of shoes, one pair of glasses, and one cup of coffee at a time.

In the heart of Guatemala, a mother shared her touching story, recounting how the simple act of receiving shoes from TOMS transformed her children's lives. These shoes did more than just protect her children's feet from diseases prevalent in their community; they served as a key to education. With these shoes, her children could attend school consistently, paving the way to a future filled with hope and possibilities far beyond what seemed attainable before. Halfway across the world, in various developing countries, individuals have voiced their profound gratitude towards the life-altering eye care provided by TOMS' eyewear program. These testimonials shed light on the cascading effects of vision care in enhancing the quality of life. The ability to see clearly not only empowers individuals in their daily tasks but also opens up new opportunities for learning and working, fundamentally changing their trajectory in life.

Further amplifying TOMS' global impact are the narratives emerging from communities that have benefitted from TOMS Roasting Co.'s clean water projects. Access to clean water is a fundamental human need, and yet, for many, it remains out of reach. The stories from these communities reiterate the need to have transformative reliable solutions to reliable resources. It's a catalyst for change, impacting various aspects of community life, from improving overall health and hygiene to enabling economic development and empowering communities to build a sustainable future. These stories collectively create the ripple effect of TOMS' One for One program, showcasing how targeted philanthropic efforts can yield substantial, life-changing benefits for individuals and communities alike. By focusing on essential needs such as shoes, vision care, and water, TOMS makes a tangible difference with a far-reaching impact. Ultimately, These success stories stand as powerful evidence of TOMS' unwavering commitment towards its mission of improving the lives of others through compassionate giving. So while TOMS has undoubtedly made significant strides in fulfilling their vision for a better tomorrow, there is always more that can be done to create a world where everyone has an equal opportunity to thrive.

Key Takeaways and Concluding Thoughts

TOMS's One for One program is a revolutionary philanthropic initiative that has had a profound impact on individuals and communities in need. By addressing fundamental needs like shoes, vision care, and water, TOMS is able to make a tangible difference while also promoting long-term sustainability and self-sufficiency. Through their efforts, TOMS has shown the power of targeted giving and how it can create lasting change for those who need it most. Their success stories serve as powerful reminders of the importance of compassion and altruism in creating a better world. But there are still many challenges facing underserved communities around the globe, and it's up to all of us to continue supporting organizations like TOMS in their mission. Every effort, no matter how small, can make a difference in the lives of underserved communities.

Reflective Questions For You, the Reader

- How can we use targeted giving to create lasting change in underserved communities?

- In what ways does TOMS promote sustainability and self-sufficiency?

- Why is it important for individuals and organizations to support initiatives like TOMS?

- How can small actions, such as purchasing a pair of shoes from TOMS, have a larger impact on the world?

- What are some other examples of successful targeted giving efforts that have had lasting effects on underserved communities?

Ben & Jerry's progressive values

Since its inception, this ice cream brand has been vocal about their support for social justice, environmental sustainability, and fair trade practices. Through advocacy campaigns and partnerships with non-profit organizations, they have built a loyal following of consumers who appreciate their values-driven approach. Ben & Jerry's, a prominent ice cream brand recognized globally, has successfully established a distinct position in the highly competitive food industry. This remarkable achievement stems not only from its array of mouth-watering and innovative flavors that captivate taste buds around the world but also from its unwavering dedication to social responsibility and environmental sustainability. This in-depth case study explores the core progressive values that are Ben & Jerry's ethos, meticulously examining how these principles have not only shaped its business operations but also significantly contributed to its positive impact on community welfare and global environmental practices.

Ben & Jerry's commitment to these values has provided it with a substantial competitive edge, allowing the company to distinguish itself in a crowded market. By appealing to a consumer base that prioritizes ethical and sustainable business practices alongside high-quality products, Ben & Jerry's has fostered a loyal customer following. The brand's innovative approach to flavor creation, combined with its active engagement in social issues and efforts to minimize its environmental footprint, has resonated deeply with consumers who seek to support companies that align with their values. Their social and environmental initiatives, such as its sourcing of fair-trade ingredients, efforts to reduce greenhouse gas emissions, and active participation in social justice movements exemplify the company's commitment to making a tangible difference in the world, beyond just selling ice cream.

Social Responsibility

Ben & Jerry's is dedicated to sourcing fair trade ingredients, which ensures that farmers and producers in developing countries receive a fair and equitable price for their goods. This commitment extends to improving livelihoods and fostering sustainable development in these communities.

Environmental Sustainability

Understanding the impact of business on the planet, the company is fervently committed to reducing its carbon footprint. This is achieved through sustainable business practices, including the use of eco-friendly packaging materials and efforts to minimize waste in their production processes. Ben & Jerry's also invests in renewable energy projects to offset its environmental impact.

Community Engagement

Beyond their environmental and social commitments, Ben & Jerry's actively participates in community initiatives, supporting a wide range of causes from environmental protection to social equality and justice. The company doesn't just donate funds; it leverages its brand and platform to raise awareness and drive action on critical issues, aligning its business operations with its mission to make the world a better place. Through these actions, Ben & Jerry's sets a powerful example for how businesses can be a force for good, blending profit with purpose to impact the world positively, *tastefully*.

Impact on Business

These core values of social and environmental responsibility have deeply influenced Ben & Jerry's brand image, nurturing a positive reputation that magnetically attracts consumers who are keenly aware of societal and environmental issues. This alignment of values has cultivated a strong, loyal customer base that not only appreciates but actively supports the company's dedicated efforts towards making the world a better place.

The sales of fair trade products under Ben & Jerry's banner have experienced a noticeable increase, a testament to the fact that consumers not only support but deeply value the company's steadfast commitment to social responsibility. This uptick in sales reflects a growing consumer desire to engage with brands that prioritize ethical standards and fair practices in their sourcing and business models.

Ben & Jerry's environmental initiatives have led to a substantial reduction in greenhouse gas emissions and waste production. This showcases the company's commitment to sustainability and its proactive approach in addressing climate change. These efforts demonstrate how they are leading by example in the corporate

world, proving that businesses can thrive while positively
impacting the planet.

Through these actions, Ben & Jerry's has established itself as more
than just an ice cream company; it has become a leading figure in
corporate responsibility, setting high standards for how businesses
can contribute to societal and environmental betterment.

Impact on Community

Ben & Jerry's active role in community engagement initiatives
has significantly fortified its reputation as a socially responsible
company, while also sparking substantial positive change within
communities. Through organizing and participating in a wide
array of events focused on pressing environmental and social
issues, Ben & Jerry's has gone above and beyond the traditional
corporate role. This proactive stance has fostered a robust sense
of shared values among its customer base, effectively creating a
community united not just by consumer preferences, but by a
deep commitment to making the world a better place overall.
Their efforts demonstrate a powerful model of how businesses
can deeply engage with their communities and work towards
common goals, extending the impact of their initiatives far beyond
traditional consumerism and into the realm of genuine social
change.

Lessons for Other Businesses

Ben & Jerry's stands out as an exemplary case for businesses striving to embed progressive values within their operational model and overall brand message. The company's commitment to social and environmental issues, alongside its dedication to producing high-quality ice cream, demonstrates how aligning business practices with ethical values not only secures a loyal consumer base but also fosters respect across the market and moves the industry forward. The key lesson here is that adherence to core values is not just a moral choice but a strategic one as well. This approach can lead to significant business achievements and catalyze positive changes across industries, showing that profitability and social responsibility feed one another.

Competitive Advantage

Ben & Jerry's unwavering commitment to upholding its progressive values not only sets it apart in the marketplace but also furnishes it with a considerable competitive advantage, achieved through several key strategies.

—**Establishing the brand as a preeminent leader** in social consciousness among consumers, thereby differentiating it in a crowded market. This unique positioning captivates customers who are eager to support businesses that reflect their own values and concerns for global issues.

—**Engaging a deeply loyal customer base** through shared
values and ethical practices. By aligning its business operations
with the principles of fairness, sustainability, and social justice,
Ben & Jerry's fosters a sense of community and belonging
among its consumers, encouraging repeated patronage and strong
word-of-mouth advocacy.

—**Influencing industry standards and practices** through
leadership in corporate responsibility. Ben & Jerry's doesn't just
follow best practices; it sets new benchmarks for ethical business
conduct, challenging peers and competitors alike to elevate their
operations in service of a greater good. This leadership role further
enhances its stature and influence in the business community.

—**Attracting motivated employees** who are aligned with the
company's mission and values. By prioritizing social impact
alongside profit, Ben & Jerry's draws talent that is not only skilled
but also passionately committed to the brand's ethos. This results
in a workforce that is highly engaged, innovative, and dedicated to
driving the company's success.

Overall, Ben & Jerry's approach to integrating its progressive
values into every aspect of its business operations is a great
example of the power behind ethical business practices. Not only
does it achieve financial success, but it also makes a positive
impact on society, setting a noteworthy example for others
to follow. Ben & Jerry's commitment to social responsibility,
environmental sustainability, and community engagement has not

only affirmed its position as a leading socially conscious brand but also demonstrated the feasibility of aligning business success with progressive values. Through its actions and initiatives, Ben & Jerry's has illustrated that ethical business practices can lead to lasting impacts on both business growth and community welfare, offering vital lessons for businesses across the globe.

Key Takeaways and Concluding Thoughts

Ben & Jerry's story serves as a powerful example of how a business can prioritize social responsibility and still achieve success. By staying true to their values and incorporating them into every aspect of their operations, Ben & Jerry's has shown that it is possible to create positive change while also running a profitable company.

One key takeaway from Ben & Jerry's is the importance of transparency and authenticity in building trust with consumers. By openly sharing their sourcing practices, supply chain processes, and philanthropic efforts, the brand has fostered strong relationships with customers who value ethical business practices.

Another important lesson from Ben & Jerry's is the impact of community engagement and giving back. Through partnerships with local organizations and grassroots movements, the company has been able to make a tangible difference in the communities where they operate.

Reflective Questions For You, the Reader

- Can you think of other grassroots campaigns that have had such success?

- How did they build support and create change?

- As a reader, have you ever considered the sourcing practices or ethical values of the companies whose products you buy? Knowing that Ben & Jerry's prioritizes these values, do you feel more inclined to support their brand?

- What are your thoughts on brands embracing political positions?

Dove's Real Beauty campaign

Launched by Dove, a brand internationally acclaimed for its extensive range of beauty products, the Real Beauty campaign emerged as a pioneering initiative that sought to radically redefine societal beauty norms. Spearheaded with the *explicit intention* of challenging the beauty industry's often restrictive and unrealistic standards, Dove embarked on a commendable mission. Through this campaign, Dove aimed to celebrate the diversity of beauty in all its forms and to promote a sense of confidence and self-esteem among women and girls across the globe. By showcasing a wide variety of body types, ages, and ethnic backgrounds in their advertisements, Dove sought to send a powerful message that beauty comes in many forms and that all women should feel celebrated and confident in their own skin. This groundbreaking campaign sparked a global conversation about beauty standards and the harmful impact they can have on individuals' self-esteem, especially women. It also served as a reminder that brands hold significant power in shaping societal perceptions and promoting positive change. Ultimately, Dove's Real Beauty campaign stands as an inspiring example of how personal branding can extend beyond individual efforts to make a meaningful impact on society.

Campaign Goals

The Real Beauty campaign set out with ambitious, multifaceted goals targeted at redefining traditional beauty standards. Its mission was to challenge societal norms and promote a more inclusive, diverse vision of beauty. By fostering a culture of self-love and acceptance, the campaign sought to empower women to embrace their unique appearances and recognize their worth beyond physical attributes. It also intended to spark a global conversation about the concept of beauty, encouraging communities worldwide to broaden their perspectives and rethink what beauty truly means. At the same time, the campaign reinforced Dove's role as a champion of real beauty and self-esteem, demonstrating the brand's commitment to building confidence and positivity through its messaging and products.

Impact Assessment

The campaign significantly altered the perception of Dove in the
eyes of consumers, rebranding it as a champion of inclusivity
and diversity. By advocating for a broader definition of beauty,
Dove not only solidified consumer trust but also significantly
increased engagement with its brand. This strategic shift not
only benefited Dove's market position but also set a new
standard for social responsibility within the beauty industry,
encouraging other companies to follow suit. To realize its
objectives, Dove implemented a series of deeply strategic measures.
Leveraging expertise from a diverse range of fields, including
psychology, marketing, and sociology, the campaign is built
upon a foundation of substantive, multi-faceted research. This
research not only informs its strategies and objectives but also
ensures that the initiatives address the complex and nuanced
factors influencing self-esteem and societal beauty standards. By
combining insights from these disciplines, the campaign takes
a well-rounded approach to empower individuals and drive
meaningful change.

Utilizing a dynamic media approach, the campaign employs
a combination of television, print, digital, and social media
platforms to maximize its reach and impact. This multi-channel
strategy ensures widespread dissemination, engaging with a
broad and diverse audience. Whether through an eye-catching
advertisement on TV, a thought-provoking article in a magazine,

or a viral post on social media, the campaign creates touchpoints that resonate with individuals from all walks of life. Introducing the Dove Self-Esteem Project as a cornerstone of the initiative, the campaign directly targets young people to educate them about the importance of self-esteem. Offering a rich array of resources, such as interactive guides, educational workshops, and online tools, the project seeks to foster a positive self-image and equip youth with the skills to navigate societal pressures with confidence. By fostering early intervention, the project aims to lay the groundwork for long-term positive change in how young people view themselves.

Collaborating with real women and influencers across a variety of platforms, the campaign creates relatable, authentic, and diverse narratives that challenge traditional beauty stereotypes. These women come from different backgrounds, ethnicities, sizes, and abilities, painting a more inclusive picture of beauty. By sharing their stories and experiences, they foster a sense of connection and relatability, empowering audiences to see beauty in a new and more inclusive way. Promoting an open discourse on beauty standards via social media channels, the campaign builds a supportive community that encourages dialogue and the sharing of personal stories. Engaging hashtags, live discussions, and interactive content invite individuals to challenge and redefine societal norms around beauty. By creating a safe space for honest conversations, the campaign not only amplifies voices but also inspires a collective movement toward a more diverse and accepting view of beauty.

Comparative Analysis

When compared with other notable campaigns like Always' #LikeAGirl, which challenges stereotypes about women in sports; Aerie's #AerieREAL, which promotes unretouched photos of women to encourage body positivity; Cover Girl's #IAmWhatIMakeUp, emphasizing personal expression through makeup; and Special K's 'Own It,' encouraging women to embrace their figures without focusing on the scale, Dove's Real Beauty campaign distinctly shines for its trailblazing approach towards inclusivity and its profound influence on shifting the beauty industry's narrative towards a more inclusive and diverse representation of beauty. Dove's initiative has not only challenged the conventional standards of beauty but also sparked a global conversation about real beauty, self-acceptance, and the importance of representation–setting a precedent for future campaigns in the industry.

Emotional Impact

The emotional resonance of the campaign was deeply rooted in several key elements that together created a powerful impact. The campaign's focus on real women with diverse body types and features instantly struck a chord with viewers who were used to seeing only one narrow definition of beauty in media.

By showcasing women of different ages, races, and sizes, Dove shattered the unrealistic expectations set by traditional beauty standards and gave a voice to those who had long been marginalized. The use of real and unretouched images added authenticity to the campaign, making it more relatable to everyday women. This contrasted with heavily edited and airbrushed images that have become the norm in advertising, creating an immediate connection with viewers and challenging them to rethink their own perceptions of beauty.

Empowerment

Central to the campaign was the idea of empowerment. It fostered a profound sense of liberation among its audience, encouraging individuals to embrace self-love and boost their confidence. The message was clear: everyone has the right to feel powerful and in control of their own self-image.

Inclusivity

Another cornerstone of the campaign was its commitment to inclusivity. By featuring a wide array of real women from different backgrounds, ages, and body types, it broke the mold of traditional beauty standards. This approach made a vast demographic feel valued and represented, nurturing the beauty in diversity.

Authenticity

Authenticity was a key driver of the campaign's success.
The genuine stories shared by participants and the brand's
commitment to challenging and changing beauty norms struck
a deep chord with many. This authenticity helped in building
a strong sense of trust and loyalty among the audience, as they
felt connected to the brand's mission on a personal level.

Engagement

The campaign went beyond simple representation; it actively
invited the audience to share their stories and experiences. This
cultivated a highly participatory and inclusive environment
where individuals felt seen and heard. Engagement became
a two-way street, with the audience contributing to the
campaign's narrative and impact.

Hope and Inspiration

The campaign offered more than just a critique of current
beauty standards; it offered a vision for a more accepting and
diverse future. It stood as a pillar of hope and inspiration,
motivating many to advocate for change and to envision a
world where everyone can feel beautiful and accepted.

Together, these elements crafted a compelling message that resonated on an emotional level, driving the campaign's success and leaving a lasting impact on its audience.

Lessons Learned

The success of Dove's campaign pinpoints the importance of authenticity, inclusivity, and engagement in crafting marketing initiatives. Future endeavors can draw from their approach to foster meaningful connections with their audience, challenge societal norms, and drive positive change. Dove's Real Beauty campaign not only achieved its goals but also made an indelible mark on the beauty industry and society at large. It remains a quintessential example of how brands can wield their influence to champion real change and uplift women worldwide.

Key Takeaways and Concluding Thoughts

Dove's Real Beauty campaign serves as a reminder of the power of purpose-driven marketing. Their Real Beauty campaign continues to inspire and influence marketers worldwide by setting an example of how purpose-driven initiatives can create meaningful connections with consumers.

Reflective Questions For You, the Reader

- Does your business or position give you the opportunity to focus on a purpose besides just the company's profits?

- What are some examples of successful purpose-driven campaigns that have resonated with you? How did they impact your perception of the brand and their products?

- In what ways can companies use their platform and resources to create positive change in society, specifically for women? How can brands uplift and empower women through their messaging and actions?

Strategies for Integrating Social Responsibility into Your Brand

Implementing social responsibility into your brand is both a noble and strategic business move. Here, I provide practical advice on identifying initiatives that align with your brand values, crafting compelling narratives around your social impact, and measuring the effectiveness of your efforts. With a clear understanding from these case studies, this section serves as a roadmap for brands looking to make a positive difference without sacrificing profitability.

Define your brand values

To successfully weave social responsibility into the fabric of your brand, the initial step involves pinpointing your foundational values. Begin this process by conducting a thorough examination of your brand's essence—what it represents, the principles it stands on, and the specific impact you wish to have on the world.

Consider what makes your brand unique and how these unique qualities can contribute to making a positive difference. This introspective journey is crucial for aligning your business practices with your desire to effect meaningful change.

Align with a cause that resonates with your values

Identifying and aligning with a cause that mirrors your brand's core values—be it environmental sustainability, social justice, or community building—not only reflects a commitment to these ideals but also enhances your brand's authenticity. By choosing a cause that aligns closely with your brand's mission, you ensure a genuine connection and dedication to the cause, which can significantly influence your audience's perception and loyalty. This strategic alignment allows your brand to make a meaningful impact while fostering a deep sense of trust and integrity among your customers.

Incorporate social responsibility into your business operations

It's crucial to think about ways to integrate social responsibility into the core of your business practices. This could involve using sustainable materials in your products or services, ensuring that your supply chain adheres to fair trade policies, or even adopting environmentally friendly manufacturing processes. By doing so, you not only contribute positively to society and the environment but also set a commendable example for others in your industry.

Communicate your impact effectively

Leverage the power of storytelling and compelling visuals to vividly showcase your brand's social impact. It's crucial to connect with consumers on an emotional level by sharing compelling narratives that represent the positive change your brand is making in the community or environment. By doing so, you'll not only strengthen consumer loyalty but also deepen their emotional connection with your brand, making them more likely to support and advocate for your mission. This strategy is an effective way to differentiate your brand in a crowded marketplace.

Measure and track your progress

It's essential to set specific, measurable goals for your social responsibility initiatives from the outset. By doing so, you can systematically evaluate the impact your actions are having over time. Regular assessment through quantitative and qualitative metrics not only helps in gauging the effectiveness of your current efforts but also serves as a critical tool for gathering insights. These analytics are invaluable for refining strategies and improving outcomes for future initiatives. Tracking progress meticulously ensures that your commitment to social responsibility translates into tangible benefits, thereby enhancing the overall value and impact of your efforts.

By following these strategies, brands can effectively integrate social responsibility into their marketing strategies and make a positive impact in the world. As seen through our case studies, purpose-driven branding not only creates loyal customers but also helps drive meaningful change in communities and industries. So why wait? Start implementing social responsibility into your brand today and be a part of creating a better tomorrow. Overall, purpose-driven branding is not just a trend, but a necessary approach for businesses that want to thrive in the ever-changing market landscape while making a positive impact on society and the environment. By staying true to your values and integrating social responsibility into your brand, you can build a strong and authentic identity that resonates with consumers and stands the test of time.

Actionable Steps

To start your purpose-driven branding journey, consider these actionable steps:

1. **Start by conducting a thorough audit** of your brand's existing values and operational practices. This process involves closely examining how your brand currently aligns with its core values and identifying specific areas where there could be a stronger connection. Look for opportunities to enhance your brand's impact on your target audience and the wider community by pinpointing areas that need improvement or greater strategic focus.

2. **Carefully select social responsibility initiatives** that

seamlessly align with your brand's core values and mission, placing a strong emphasis on making authentic contributions that have a real impact. Avoid engaging in superficial gestures that are merely for show; instead, aim for actions that genuinely resonate with your brand and its audience, fostering a deeper connection and making a meaningful difference in the community.

3. **Develop a compelling brand story** that seamlessly connects your brand's core values to its actions, emphasizing the importance of transparency and consistency in all forms of communication. This approach fosters trust and builds a stronger bond with your audience, making it essential for a coherent and authentic brand experience.

4. **To effectively implement this change, it's crucial to engage your entire organization**, fostering a culture that not only supports but also actively lives out your brand's core values. This involves clear communication, training, and perhaps most importantly, leading by example to ensure that every member of your team understands and is aligned with these values.

5. **Make it a priority** to periodically evaluate and report on the impact your actions have on your goals. Utilize these valuable testing skills to fine-tune your strategy and reinforce your brand's dedication to driving

significant change. This ongoing process of assessment and adaptation is crucial for deepening the effectiveness of your brand's commitment to making a meaningful difference.

Reflective Questions For You, the Reader

- Reflect on your brand's core values. How are these currently manifested in your operations, and where could you improve?

- Consider the case studies from this chapter. Which aspects of their purpose-driven approaches resonate with your brand's goals, and how can you adapt these lessons to your context?

- What immediate actions can your brand take to integrate social responsibility more fully into its strategy and operations?

- How will you measure the success of your brand's purpose-driven initiatives, and what steps can you take to ensure continuous improvement and greater impact?

7

Embracing Vulnerability

In a world that often equates vulnerability with weakness, Chapter seven invites you to reconsider the stigma. It proposes a compelling argument for vulnerability as a formidable strength particularly within the realms of business and branding. By weaving together key concepts, real-life case studies, personal anecdotes, and actionable steps, this chapter outlines a path toward a more authentic, connected, and successful professional life.

Everyday Examples of Vulnerability in Leadership

—**The Tech Startup Founder**: This leader pioneered a culture of transparency and resilience by openly sharing their own mistakes and failures. Rather than shrouding errors in secrecy, they championed the idea that failure was not something to be feared but rather a necessary step towards innovation and growth. This approach not only bolstered trust among the team members but also inspired them to embrace calculated risks. The outcome was a more dynamic, innovative team that achieved breakthroughs and success, transforming the way startups approach failure and risk-taking.

—**The Corporate Executive**: By courageously acknowledging their personal struggles with mental health, this leader did more than just humanize themselves—they actively tore down the stigma surrounding mental health issues in the corporate environment. This act of honesty fostered a culture of support and openness within the company, significantly improving overall employee well-being and productivity. It led to the implementation of more robust mental health support systems and encouraged a dialogue about work-life balance, setting a precedent for other companies to follow.

—**The School Principal**: In a bold move, this principal demonstrated the power of vulnerability by admitting when they were wrong in front of the entire school. This action set a powerful precedent within the educational environment, paving the way for open communication and mutual respect between staff and students. By leading through example, the principal created a learning environment where continuous improvement was the collective goal. This approach encouraged both staff and students to embrace their mistakes as learning opportunities, fostering a culture of growth and mutual support.

Key Concepts Explored

Professionalism and Personal Authenticity

This chapter explores how to balance professionalism with personal authenticity, showing how staying true to yourself can boost both credibility and relatability while upholding professional standards.

The Power of Vulnerability

As you read through this chapter, imagine the transformative impact of unveiling your authentic self in both leadership and branding. Discover how being vulnerable can cultivate genuine connections, leading to a more engaging and relatable presence.

Strategies for Connection

Use this chapter to uncover effective strategies to leverage vulnerability as a tool to build trust, foster collaboration, and create deeper, more meaningful relationships in your workplace. Explore practical tips and techniques that turn vulnerability into a strength, promoting a culture of openness and teamwork.

Concepts from Brené Brown's Research

In today's fast-paced and often unforgiving world of business, the conventional image of a leader is someone who is assertive, unyielding, and infallible. However, Dr. Brené Brown's groundbreaking research has paved the way for a revolutionary understanding of leadership—one that embraces vulnerability and acknowledges shame not as weaknesses, but as a powerful tool for building more authentic, empathetic, and effective leaders.

Vulnerability

At the core of Brené Brown's influential work lies a transformative idea: vulnerability serves as the foundation for innovation, creativity, and change. Moving away from the conventional perspective that often equates vulnerability with weakness, Brown's research presents a compelling argument for its necessity in building robust, meaningful connections and cultivating a sense of trust among team members. By embracing vulnerability, leaders can become more accessible and relatable figures, thereby creating a workplace atmosphere that champions open communication and mutual respect. This approach not only helps in breaking down barriers and fostering a culture of inclusivity but also empowers individuals to share their ideas and perspectives fearlessly, leading to a more dynamic and innovative team environment. In a world that frequently prioritizes strength and certainty, Brown's work is a vital reminder of the power and potential that vulnerability holds in enabling personal growth and driving collective progress.

Shame

Closely linked with the concept of vulnerability is the powerful
emotion of shame, which plays a significant role in hindering
individuals from achieving their fullest potential. Brené Brown's
extensive research sheds light on the critical importance of
recognizing and effectively addressing feelings of shame. This
recognition is not just for personal growth but also for
fostering a leadership style that is both compassionate and
emotionally intelligent. Brown advocates for leaders to cultivate
an environment where vulnerability is not seen as a weakness
but as a strength, thereby encouraging a more authentic and
productive workplace. This approach to leadership and personal
development emphasizes the need for emotional intelligence in
creating stronger, more resilient individuals and organizations.

Applying Brown's Findings to Your Leadership Practice

Leaders looking to implement Brown's teachings can start
with self-reflection and vulnerability. It's important to recognize
that being vulnerable does not equate to weakness, but rather
demonstrates courage and authenticity. As leaders, it's crucial to
acknowledge mistakes and take ownership of them, rather than
deflecting or blaming others. This builds trust and begins to
create a safe space for open communication within the workplace
which is vital for fostering collaboration. By actively listening to
employees' ideas and concerns without judgement, encouraging

feedback and constructive criticism, and demonstrating empathy towards their experiences, we can create an environment that promotes success for everyone.

Foster Openness

Openly share your own experiences of failure and growth. By doing so, you not only humanize yourself in the eyes of your team members but also signal to them that it's safe to share their own struggles and learning moments. This fosters a culture of transparency and builds a solid foundation of trust within your team, encouraging a more cohesive and open work environment.

Practice Empathy

Lead every interaction with understanding and compassion. Make it a point to acknowledge both the personal and professional struggles your team members might be facing. Address these challenges in an open and supportive manner, showing that you not only recognize their efforts but are also there to support them through their ups and downs. This empathetic leadership style helps in creating a supportive atmosphere where team members feel valued and understood.

Cherish Feedback

Treat feedback as a golden opportunity for personal and professional growth. By welcoming constructive criticism with open arms and a positive attitude, you underline the idea that being vulnerable and receptive to feedback is a strength, rather than a weakness. This approach encourages a culture of continuous improvement, where everyone feels empowered to speak up and contribute to mutual growth.

Lead by Example

Demonstrating vulnerability might seem daunting at first, but by actively doing so, you set a powerful precedent that it's perfectly okay not to have all the answers. This act of courage shows your team that vulnerability leads to growth and learning, which in turn fosters a resilient and closely-knit team atmosphere. Such a team, comfortable in its collective vulnerability, becomes capable of overcoming challenges together and emerging stronger on the other side.

Brené Brown's exploration into vulnerability and shame has indeed revolutionized our understanding of effective leadership. It challenges the archetype of the stoic, impenetrable leader, proposing instead that true leadership strength lies in the ability to be vulnerable and connect genuinely with others. For leadership professionals, business owners, and team managers, adopting this innovative approach could transform not just their personal leadership style but the very fabric of their organizations. In a world that often values superficial toughness, the bravest thing a leader can do is to open up, revealing that the path to true strength and effective leadership is paved with vulnerability and a willingness to confront shame.

Authentic Branding: The Honest Company's Blueprint for Success

In today's world, where consumers face a barrage of choices and marketing claims, The Honest Company emerges as a promise of authenticity and trust. Co-founded by actress and entrepreneur Jessica Alba, the brand distinguishes itself by its unwavering commitment to offering safe, effective, and environmentally friendly products specifically designed for families. This commitment is deeply rooted in Alba's own journey as a mother, motivated by her desire to find products that she could trust for her children's health and well-being. Her personal quest for better, safer products led to the foundation of The Honest Company, which has since become a symbol of integrity in the marketplace. This narrative of genuine concern and proactive solution-seeking forms the framework of the brand, offering consumers not just products, but a reflection of a mother's care and dedication.

Unveiling the Core of Authentic Engagement

Authenticity in branding isn't merely a strategy; it's a dedicated approach that The Honest Company has perfected, nurturing a deep sense of loyalty among its customer base. This unique approach has allowed them to stand out in a crowded marketplace by being transparent and genuine in every aspect of their business. From their product development to marketing, The Honest Company emphasizes honesty and integrity, resonating with consumers who value these traits. Looking closer we can see how they've achieved such a strong connection with their audience using a well defined methodology.

Personal Connection

Alba's compelling story and the heartfelt motivation behind founding The Honest Company deeply connect with its primary audience—parents who desire nothing but the best for their children. This connection is a stellar example of how companies can ground themselves in relatable, human narratives that echo their core values and vision, making it more than just about selling products; it's about sharing a journey that many can relate to and find inspiration in.

Transparency

By openly sharing its trials and transformations, especially during its formative years, The Honest Company has crafted a narrative rich in growth and resilience. This level of honesty about the challenges faced and the steadfast commitment to overcoming them not only humanizes the brand but significantly bolsters consumer trust. It showcases a journey of evolution and dedication to principles, inviting consumers to be a part of the story.

Social Media Savvy

The strategic use of social media platforms to share behind-the-scenes content, such as exclusive media content showcasing their product manufacturing and rigorous safety testing, has effectively demystified these processes. This approach fosters a stronger sense of community and trust among followers. By pulling back the curtain on these operations, The Honest Company offers a transparent look into its brand operations and values, engaging consumers with the authenticity and integrity of its processes.

Feedback-Focused

Placing a high value on customer feedback, The Honest Company actively addresses concerns and queries in a public and transparent manner. This open dialogue punctuates the brand's genuine care for the consumer experience and wellbeing, which in turn, strengthens consumer loyalty. It's a testament to the company's commitment to not just meeting but exceeding customer expectations, building a foundation of trust and respect.

Consistency is Key

By ensuring that its messaging and branding remain consistent across all communication platforms, The Honest Company effectively reinforces its core values at every possible touchpoint. This strategy presents a unified and authentic brand identity to the world. Whether it's through marketing materials, social media posts, or direct customer service interactions, the company consistently communicates its dedication to honesty, quality, and transparency, solidifying its position as a trusted household name. Here's an in-depth look at how other brands can incorporate The Honest Company's successful strategies into their own business models for enhanced outcomes.

Understand Your Audience

To foster an authentic connection, it's crucial to deeply comprehend the needs, concerns, and aspirations of your target audience. This goes beyond surface-level understanding; it requires a genuine immersion into what truly matters to them, recognizing that addressing these aspects can build a strong, emotional bond.

Journey Sharing

Authentic storytelling is about being courageous enough to share your brand's journey, including the highs and the lows. This approach involves vulnerability, allowing your audience to see the real challenges and triumphs behind your brand. Such transparency can significantly deepen connections as it invites your audience to be part of your story.

Behind-the-Scenes Transparency

In today's digital age, utilizing platforms to share the inner workings of your brand can foster a deeper trust and connection. This could encompass everything from the nuances of product creation to your brand's commitment to ethical sourcing and sustainability. By pulling back the curtain, you instill confidence and trust in your audience, showing them what stands behind the products or services they love.

Actively Engage with Feedback

Viewing customer feedback as an invaluable resource is key. Actively addressing and engaging with this feedback in an open manner not only helps in improving your offerings but also signifies a strong commitment to your audience's satisfaction. It shows that you value their input and are dedicated to evolving based on their needs and experiences.

Maintain Messaging Cohesion

Consistency is king when it comes to authenticity. Ensuring that your brand's voice, values, and visual identity are coherent and aligned across all channels fortifies this authenticity. This cohesion makes your brand's message more powerful, believable, and resonant with your audience. It's about creating a seamless experience that reinforces your brand's core essence at every touchpoint.

Emotional Storytelling At The Heart of Authenticity

The Honest Company skillfully utilizes emotional storytelling to foster a deep connection with its audience. From sharing Jessica Alba's motivation to expansive customer journeys, the brand effectively employs emotional triggers such as trust, empathy, and belonging. These elements resonate on a profound level, compelling individuals to become part of a community that shares their values and aspirations.

True authenticity in branding hinges on principles like transparency, honesty, connection, consistency, and ethical practices. Emotional storytelling serves as a conduit for these values, engaging audiences in a meaningful dialogue rooted in shared experiences and mutual trust.

Engaging Through Emotional Triggers

For brands aiming to harness the power of authenticity, focusing on emotional triggers such as trust, empathy, and a sense of belonging is crucial. These elements not only captivate but also build a lasting relationship with the audience, transforming customers into brand advocates. In essence, The Honest Company exemplifies how authenticity can pave the way for a powerful and trustworthy brand presence. By integrating these methods into your branding strategy, you can cultivate a genuine connection with your audience and grow together.

Personal Anecdotes

From sharing personal challenges at a conference to disclosing a professional setback to team members, these stories exemplify the unexpected power and positive outcomes that can emerge from vulnerability. They serve as evidence that when business leaders and brands open up, they can engender trust, loyalty, and authentic engagement.

The Incident That Put My Resilience to the Test

My moment of reckoning came unexpectedly during a highly anticipated product launch event for my new app. Amid the excitement, a major programming error caused the app to malfunction spectacularly in front of a live audience comprised of media, stakeholders, and potential customers. The room, buzzing with anticipation seconds before, was suddenly fraught with disappointment and murmurs of concern. In a situation that had the potential to spiral into a significant public relations disaster, I took a decisive and courageous step. Understanding the gravity of the moment, I chose to confront the issue directly by stepping onto the stage and bravely addressing the elephant in the room head-on, demonstrating leadership and transparency.

The reaction from the audience was both unexpected and remarkable. Instead of disappointment or criticism, there was an outpouring of support and empathy for my brand. The vulnerability shown in that moment not only diffused a potentially damaging situation but also earned me respect and admiration from my customers and stakeholders. With an audience braced for excuses or perhaps a hasty attempt to downplay the situation, I chose instead to be entirely transparent. Admitting to the mistake candidly, I detailed what went wrong, why it happened, and, most importantly, how I intended to rectify it. This honest admission was a gamble, one that could only be taken by someone who understood the inexplicable value of trust in the delicate relationship between a brand and its community. The audience's emotional trajectory moved from disappointment and concern to empathy, support, and renewed confidence in my brand. Through admitting my vulnerability, I inadvertently humanized the brand, making it more relatable and trustworthy.

Client Feedback

Reflecting on the recent incident, I was pleasantly surprised by the overwhelmingly positive feedback from users and attendees. It offered a fresh perspective on the situation and reinforced the importance of authenticity. "I've never felt so connected to a brand before," shared Alex, a long-time app user. This sentiment was particularly striking given the circumstances. Jamie, who attended one of our major events, remarked, "Seeing them own up to a mistake and work hard to make it right? That's what builds real loyalty." These words underline the power of accountability in fostering trust and connection. Sam, another user, perfectly captured the collective sentiment: "I feel like we're on the same team." This sense of solidarity is something I deeply value and strive to nurture. Moments like these remind me that building genuine relationships with our users goes far beyond the app—it's about creating a shared journey.

These heartfelt responses strengthen the importance of my decision to be transparent about the incident, coupled with my sincere commitment to continuous improvement. Far from weakening the brand in the eyes of my followers, this approach has, in fact, fortified it, demonstrating the strength that can come from vulnerability and the power of turning challenges into opportunities for strengthening trust within the community.

From this experience, several lessons emerged. First and foremost, the value of open communication cannot be underestimated. By sharing my journey and being transparent about my mistakes, I was able to build a stronger bond with my audience. They appreciated hearing the truth from me directly, rather than through rumors or speculation. This created a sense of trust and authenticity that ultimately strengthened our relationship.

Secondly, owning up to our mistakes can be difficult, but it is essential for growth. As leaders in any community, we must recognize that we are not infallible and are capable of making errors. However, how we handle those errors speaks volumes about our character. Taking ownership and responsibility shows humility and a willingness to learn from our mistakes. This story showcases the fact that vulnerability, often seen as a weakness, can be transformed into a source of strength and competitive advantage. It humanizes you and your brand, fostering a deeper connection with your audience that's built on mutual respect and trust.

I share this anecdote not just as a reflection of past growth but as a call to action for businesses everywhere. In a world where authenticity and transparency are increasingly valued, the courage to show vulnerability may well be the key to building lasting, loyal relationships with your customers.

Navigating Chaos with Candor: A Conference Tale

Imagine standing before an eager and expansive audience, all gathered at a prestigious high-stakes technology conference, ready to deliver a compelling keynote address that encapsulates months of relentless work, profound insights, and groundbreaking innovations. The atmosphere is electric, charged with palpable anticipation. Expectations from the audience are sky-high, mirroring the towering ambition behind your presentation. The pressure to perform flawlessly is immense, as every word and slide will be scrutinized by industry experts, peers, and potential investors, making this moment not just a presentation, but a pivotal point in your career and the trajectory of your project. The stakes couldn't be higher.

Now imagine the moment when everything begins to unravel—a technical glitch, an unexpected disruption, or maybe an overwhelming sense of stage fright. Suddenly, your carefully crafted presentation feels like a house of cards, with each slide crashing down one by one. And as fate would have it, Murphy's Law reigns supreme. Technical glitches derail the presentation setup, causing significant delays. The once eager eyes of the audience begin to betray signs of restlessness and disinterest. In those moments, my confidence seemed to crumble piece by piece, the weight of disappointment growing heavier with each passing minute. The perfect storm of professional nightmares was upon me. And as I stood there, feeling increasingly vulnerable and exposed, I realized that the only way out—was through—with candor.

As defined by Merriam-Webster, candor is "honesty or frankness in expression; freedom from bias, prejudice, or malice; fairness." In times of chaos, candor can feel like the last thing we have in our arsenal. But as I navigated through that tumultuous presentation, I discovered that embracing candor was my only chance at salvaging the situation and turning it into a success.

Faced with dwindling options, I made a choice. Instead of barreling through with a faltering spirit or retreating behind a veil of professionalism, I chose vulnerability. I took a deep breath and openly shared the cascade of emotions unraveling behind my composed façade: frustration, disappointment, and the gnawing fear of letting everyone, myself included—down.

"I'm right there with you, feeling every bit of this delay and its frustration," I admitted, my voice steadier than I felt. "I wanted this to be seamless, but sometimes, despite our best efforts, things slip beyond our grasp." And as I spoke, something shifted in the room. The once restless audience began to nod along sympathetically, their expressions softening and becoming more understanding. I had tapped into an unspoken truth—chaos is inevitable, but *how we handle it* can make all the difference.

The room's atmosphere transformed almost instantly. The air of restlessness gave way to an undeniable wave of empathy and understanding. After the talk, attendees approached me not with critiques, but with their own tales of unexpected setbacks and the resilience they discovered therein. Our shared vulnerabilities had fostered a connection far stronger than any polished presentation could.

This experience taught me an invaluable lesson about the power of vulnerability, especially in professional environments often masked by relentless perfectionism. By choosing to share my struggles, I inadvertently facilitated a deeper connection with my audience, turning potential critics into compassionate allies. The authenticity of the moment dismantled barriers, encouraging open engagement, fostering trust, and cultivating a loyal community inspired not just by success, but by the real, raw, and relatable human experience behind it. In the end, my candor had turned a potentially disastrous situation into an unforgettable moment of human connection and understanding.

In the landscapes of our professional lives, where success is often defined by precision, achievement, and unyielding strength, I encourage you to consider moments for genuine authenticity. Reflect on how transparency and vulnerability, particularly in times of challenge, can transform potential setbacks into powerful opportunities for connection and growth. We often find ourselves at the crossroads of vulnerability and professionalism; and when you do, remember, it is courage, not the absence of fear or failure, that fosters true connection and understanding.

Overcoming Setbacks Together

At the onset of our project, my team and I were buoyed by enthusiasm and a shared commitment to excellence. We had meticulously planned every phase, confident in our ability to meet the ambitious deadline set before us. However, the path to success is seldom without its obstacles, and ours came in the form of unforeseen technical issues that led to a significant delay in delivery. This setback was a result of unexpected software bugs compounded by miscommunication within our team regarding task priorities. The realization that we would not meet our deadline was not just a professional setback; it was a moment of profound disappointment and frustration for all involved.

When I disclosed the recent setback to my team, I prioritized transparency and accountability, fully aware that our approach to overcoming this challenge would significantly shape our path forward. The response from my team was nothing short of remarkable and truly exceeded my expectations. Despite the initial wave of concern that washed over the room, there was an almost instantaneous shift in attitude towards understanding the root causes of the setback. This was not about assigning blame; it was about a collective determination to identify and overcome the obstacles we faced. Together, we launched a thorough analysis of the situation, scrutinizing every detail to pinpoint where things went awry. It was a moment that not only transformed our team dynamic but also fostered an environment of open dialogue, collaboration, and mutual support. This experience reinforced the value of facing challenges head-on as a unified team, proving that with the right mindset, even setbacks can lead to significant growth and strengthening of team bonds.

We learned several vital lessons from this experience. Clear and consistent communication within the team is paramount to ensuring everyone is aligned with the project's priorities and understands their individual roles. Regular progress updates and the early identification of potential roadblocks are crucial to mitigating issues before they escalate. We also recognized the importance of having contingency plans for critical project components and the necessity of a robust testing and debugging process.

The emotional toll of this setback was significant, prompting a period of deep reflection on my part as a leader. It became abundantly clear that to navigate through such challenges, resilience, adaptability, and the ability to show vulnerabilities are not just desirable, but essential qualities in real leadership. This harrowing experience served as a turning point, reshaping my approach to leadership and exemplifying the paramount importance of fostering a proactive, supportive, and transparent team culture. As I navigated through this period of introspection, I realized that my leadership style needed a fundamental shift. It evolved to prioritize open communication, encouraging a dialogue that invites diverse perspectives and ideas. Collaboration became a cornerstone of our team's ethos, recognizing that collective effort and shared responsibility are key to achieving our objectives. I became deeply committed to the empowerment of each team member, encouraging them to take initiative and assume ownership of their work, thereby fostering a sense of accountability and personal investment in our collective success.

These changes not only enhanced our team's performance but also contributed to creating a more cohesive and motivated team environment. The lessons learned from this setback have been invaluable, teaching me that the heart of effective leadership lies in the ability to adapt, to listen, and to *empower those around you*. The journey through this unexpected challenge has only served to strengthen the team's bonds, reinforcing the vital lesson that setbacks can often be blessings in disguise when faced and overcome together.

Our collective response to this setback not only helped us overcome the immediate challenges but also strengthened our team's cohesion, accountability, and commitment to excellence.

We implemented new strategies to prevent similar setbacks, focusing on improving our communication, planning, and testing processes. The positive outcome of this challenging experience was a more resilient and collaborative team, better equipped to tackle future obstacles.

Facing a professional setback is undoubtedly challenging, but it also presents an opportunity for growth, learning, and improvement. This experience not only tested my resilience but ultimately demonstrated the strength of our team and the positive impact of adaptive leadership. It taught us that together, with clear communication, a collaborative spirit, and a commitment to continuous improvement, there's no obstacle we can't overcome. Don't be afraid to embrace setbacks as opportunities for growth and keep pushing forward on your leadership journey.

> *"A bend in the road is not the end of the road...*
> *Unless you fail to make the turn."*
> —Helen Keller

Key Takeaways and Concluding Thoughts

Demonstrating vulnerability can fundamentally alter how customers perceive a brand, paving the way for the development of deeper, more meaningful connections. By showing a more human side, businesses can foster a sense of empathy and relatability among their audience.

A brand's willingness to openly admit mistakes and take responsibility can transform potentially negative experiences into valuable opportunities for growth and trust-building. This level of transparency not only humanizes a brand but also demonstrates a commitment to integrity and improvement.

Engaging the community in the process of finding resolutions not only helps in mending issues more effectively but also significantly strengthens trust and active engagement among the customer base. This collaborative approach can lead to a more loyal and supportive community, invested in the brand's success and well-being.

Brands that dare to be vulnerable, that engage openly with their audience especially in times of adversity, stand to gain not just in terms of immediate problem-solving but in cultivating enduring trust and loyalty, the pillars upon which successful brands are built. The next time you face a setback or make an error, consider embracing vulnerability as an opportunity to showcase your authenticity and strengthen your relationship with your team or your community. Let this be a reminder that sometimes, it is in our most vulnerable moments that we *truly shine*.

Chapter seven makes a compelling case for redefining vulnerability as a source of strength in the professional realm. By integrating this trait into our professional lives, we stand not only to transform our leadership and branding strategies but to catalyze growth, inspire trust, and forge deeper connections. In the complex landscape of modern business, vulnerability might just be the secret weapon we didn't know we needed.

Actionable Steps

Embarking on a journey to embrace vulnerability in your professional life starts with a few actionable steps. These strategies can guide you, whether you're an entrepreneur building your business or aiming to strengthen your personal brand within another company.

1. **Reflect and Discover**: Take time to reflect on your past experiences where showing vulnerability led to significant positive change or personal growth. Consider moments when being open about your feelings or challenges helped forge deeper connections or opened up new opportunities.

2. **Start Small**: Begin your journey towards greater openness by sharing in environments where you feel safe and supported. Start with small acts of vulnerability in familiar settings before moving on to more significant risks in less controlled environments.

3. **Communicate with Authenticity**: When you share, be genuine about the reasons behind your actions and

decisions. It's important to also express any uncertainties or doubts you might have. Authentic communication builds trust and strengthens relationships.

4. **Share Your Story**: Use different platforms, such as blogs, social media, or public speaking opportunities, to share your experiences of failure and the lessons you've learned. Aim to connect with your audience on a human level, rather than trying to impress them with your successes.

5. **Lead by Example**: Create a culture in your personal and professional life where vulnerability is not just accepted but valued. By demonstrating vulnerability yourself, you encourage others to be open and foster a supportive environment where everyone feels safe to share.

6. **Evaluate and Adjust**: Make it a habit to regularly assess how your openness is affecting your relationships and personal growth. Be prepared to make adjustments to your approach as necessary, based on the feedback you receive and the outcomes you observe. Continual evaluation ensures that your practice of vulnerability remains healthy and constructive.

8

A New Wave of Empowerment

In recent years, we've witnessed a powerful shift that has laid the groundwork for a new era of empowerment. Across the globe, movements striving for gender equality and inclusion have gained momentum, manifesting a collective aspiration towards creating a more balanced and fair society. This chapter opens a window into contemporary female empowerment, particularly in the business sphere, and outlines actions we can all take to contribute to this burgeoning wave of change.

The State of Women's Empowerment in Business

Despite the progress made over the years, women in the business world still encounter substantial obstacles that hinder our advancement. These challenges range from unequal pay, where women are often paid less than their male counterparts for the same work, to underrepresentation in top leadership roles, creating a disparity in the decision-making processes of many organizations. Women frequently face unconscious bias and a lack of mentorship opportunities, which can impede their professional growth and development.

However, it's not all grim. Recent statistics indicate a promising increase in female entrepreneurship and leadership across various sectors. This trend suggests that more women are breaking through barriers and paving the way for future generations, signaling a gradual but significant shift toward gender equality in the business arena. As these pioneering women step into roles traditionally dominated by men, they not only contribute diverse perspectives and innovative approaches but also inspire a change in societal perceptions and corporate cultures.

The Role of Mentorship and Community

The path to success is rarely traveled alone. In the world of professional development, and particularly for women, the importance of mentorship and the presence of strong, supportive communities cannot be emphasized enough. These networks are not just social circles; they are the bedrock for the cultivation of talent, the exchange of invaluable insights, and the fostering of both personal and professional growth. Through the sharing of personal stories and rich anecdotes, the transformative impact of mentorship is brought to light, illustrating its power to change lives. Mentorship programs do much more than provide advice and support. They establish empowering environments that embolden women to chase their dreams with confidence. By bridging the gap between aspiring professionals and those with years of experience, these initiatives play a crucial role in helping women to navigate the intricate labyrinth of their careers. They tackle the challenges faced by women in the professional sphere head-on, breaking down the barriers that have historically hindered their progress and paving the way for future generations to reach new heights of success.

The benefits of such mentorship and support extend beyond the individual. They have a ripple effect, enriching the professional community as a whole. As more women ascend to leadership positions and achieve their career goals, they become role models and mentors themselves, perpetuating a cycle of empowerment and advancement. In this way, mentorship programs are not just shaping the leaders of tomorrow; they are fostering a more inclusive, equitable, and dynamic professional landscape for everyone today.

The Global Shapers Community: Empowering Young Voices

The Global Shapers Community, a vibrant initiative launched by the World Economic Forum, showcases the immense power of young individuals in propelling social change across the globe. With a special focus on the contributions of female shapers, the community demonstrates the significant role that projects centered around education, health, and equality play in creating tangible impacts within society. By tackling these crucial issues, these young leaders understand the importance of incorporating diverse perspectives and innovative approaches in addressing some of the world's most pressing challenges, thus bringing to light the potential for positive change when youth are empowered to take action.

The Global Shapers Community also emphasizes the value of mentorship and collaboration, creating a support system for these young activists to thrive in their endeavors. Through this network, they have access to resources, expertise, and guidance from experienced professionals. This not only enhances their personal development but also amplifies their impact as they work towards building a better future for all.

The #MeToo Campaign and Its Global Impact

The #MeToo movement, since its inception, has significantly magnified women's voices across the globe, shining a powerful light on the widespread issues of sexual harassment and assault. This is particularly significant in environments that previously stifled or ignored such critical conversations. Understanding the origins of the #MeToo movement provides valuable insight into its extensive influence. It began with the courageous efforts of activist Tarana Burke, who first used the term to raise awareness about sexual violence. Her work laid the foundation for what would become a global phenomenon when actress Alyssa Milano amplified the message on social media. Milano's viral tweet encouraged victims of sexual harassment and assault to share their stories, using '#MeToo' to demonstrate the ubiquity of the problem, thus propelling the movement into the global spotlight.

As we further understand the outcomes of this groundbreaking movement, it becomes evident that it has catalyzed profound changes within society and the workplace. These changes include a critical reevaluation of existing policies and cultural norms, the enactment of more stringent laws to protect individuals from sexual misconduct, and a noticeable shift in public consciousness. This shift has led to a broader and more nuanced understanding of the deeply ingrained issues of gender-based violence and discrimination.

Beyond bringing survivors together, the #MeToo movement has ignited a worldwide dialogue about consent, power dynamics, and the structural inequalities that enable sexual misconduct. It has forged a robust sense of solidarity among those affected, challenging the status quo by demanding greater accountability from individuals in positions of power and meaningful change in societal attitudes towards victims. This movement represents a pivotal moment in history, marking a significant step forward in the fight against gender-based violence and discrimination. It offers hope and empowerment to countless individuals who had previously felt isolated and voiceless, providing them with a platform to share their stories and seek justice. As the movement continues to evolve, it remains a guiding light of change, driving forward the global conversation on these critical issues and paving the way for a more inclusive and equitable society.

Actions You Can Take to Support the New Wave of Empowerment

Engagement begins with actionable, practical ways for you, the reader, to participate in the movement wave, from joining global initiatives to mentoring and sharing stories of your own experiences of empowerment. To advocating for policy changes, and encouraging young women to pursue their dreams fearlessly. The drive towards gender equality and empowerment represents a critical, collective effort that mandates active participation from every individual in society. It's not merely about acknowledging the need for equality but about taking tangible steps to make it a reality. This chapter explores the significant advancements made in the realm of gender equality, celebrates the inspiring success stories of women from various sectors, and provides a detailed roadmap of actionable steps that individuals and organizations can take to further the cause. By serving as a call to arms, it encourages everyone to contribute their share, however big or small, towards championing the cause of female empowerment and creating a more equitable world for future generations.

In a world brimming with untapped potential and burgeoning dreams, the new wave of empowerment is carrying with it a foundation of hope and strength. It champions a singular, unwavering goal: *to encourage young women to pursue their dreams fearlessly.* Across the globe, stories of resilience, courage, and transformation are unfolding, serving as a testament to the power of believing in one's self and the impact of collective support.

How You Can Empower Change

Empowerment is built from the threads of individual actions and collective endeavors. Here's how *you* can actively contribute to this vibrant movement.

Engage with Global Initiatives

Make sure to stay connected by following my social media channels. This will keep you informed about the latest opportunities to contribute to my cause. By participating in global initiatives, you become part of a larger community committed to making a difference.

Share Stories

One of the most powerful ways to inspire change is by sharing personal stories. Whether it's your own experience or that of empowered women in your circle, share these stories to illuminate the path for others. Use the designated hashtags to amplify your voice and join the chorus of voices uplifting and empowering each other.

Mentorship

Dedicate your time, insights, and support to mentor young women in your community. By offering guidance, you can help them navigate their paths and achieve their aspirations. Your mentorship can make a significant impact on their lives and contribute to their growth and success.

Advocacy

Stand in solidarity with women everywhere by advocating for gender equality. Use your voice to support policies that ensure equal access to education and opportunities for every woman, regardless of her background. Your advocacy is crucial in driving positive change and promoting fairness and justice.

Spread the Word

Take an active role in spreading the word about this movement to your friends, family, and colleagues. Encourage them to join in and contribute to building a more inclusive and supportive society. Show them how each individual action, no matter how small, contributes to the larger goal of weaving a fabric of support that uplifts everyone.

Success Stories That Inspire

Our success is not defined by the magnitude of inspiration, but by its impact.

—**Allow yourself to be motivated** by the remarkable woman who, against all conceivable odds, completed a marathon. Her achievement went beyond personal victory; it served as a catalyst, inspiring her entire community to embrace healthier living choices and prioritize their physical well-being.

—**Be galvanized by the visionary entrepreneur** whose creation of a sustainable fashion brand achieved much more than realizing her own business aspirations. Through her venture, she champions the causes of environmental sustainability and ethical labor practices, setting a new standard for the fashion industry and encouraging others to follow in her eco-friendly footsteps.

—**Be uplifted by the dedicated teacher** who, recognizing the barriers to girls' education in her country, initiated a groundbreaking campaign. Her efforts paid off, significantly boosting girls' access to education and marking a monumental step toward bridging the gender gap in educational opportunities, thereby empowering future generations of women.

—**Be empowered by the moving story of a domestic violence survivor** who, from the ashes of her past, rebuilt her life from the ground up. Today, she stands as a beacon of hope and guidance for other victims, advocating for their rights and offering the support needed to overcome their circumstances, proving that healing and strength are possible after trauma.

—Be inspired by the first-generation college graduate whose journey didn't stop at achieving her own educational goals. By mentoring young students from similar socio-economic backgrounds, she demonstrates that higher education is within their grasp, breaking cycles of poverty and setting a precedent for success against the odds, thus lighting a path for future generations to follow.

Join Global Initiatives, Together We Empower Change

Now more than ever, your voice, your story, and your actions can catalyze the change we envision for the world. By joining hands in this empowering movement, we can light up the path for countless young women, piloting them toward their dreams with unwavering support and boundless encouragement.

Engage with others on social media, share your story, and become a pillar of support in this beautiful empowerment mosaic. Together, we are unstoppable.

> *"Here's to strong women. May we know them. May we be them. May we raise them."*

—Unknown

The empowerment wave is more than just a moment; it's a movement. With each action we take, we get one step closer to a society where equality isn't just a goal, but a reality. The future is in our hands—let's make it empowering for everyone.

9

The Importance of Personal Branding

I n today's digitally driven world, personal branding has transcended the realm of marketing fluff and cemented itself as a crucial component of professional success. Whether you aim to climb the corporate ladder, cultivate a thriving business, or make a mark in any field, understanding the fundamentals of crafting and nurturing your personal brand is indispensable. This chapter will guide you through the practicalities of enhancing your personal branding efforts, offering tailored strategies that cater to varied goals—from entrepreneurship to emerging as a thought leader in the corporate domain.

The Pillars of Personal Branding

Personal branding goes beyond mere self-promotion; it's about building a reputation as a distinguished expert in your field, clearly articulating your core values, and forging authentic connections with your audience. It involves a strategic blend of showcasing your knowledge, skills, and personality in a way that resonates with others. Successful personal brands like Michelle Obama, Melinda Gates, and Oprah Winfrey stand as towering examples of this concept. They have mastered the art of aligning their public persona with their core values and vision, effectively creating a powerful and lasting image in the public consciousness.

These individuals demonstrate how personal branding can elevate one's influence and impact, turning their names into symbols of credibility, trust, and inspiration in their respective domains. Through consistent messaging, engaging storytelling, and genuine interactions, they've built legacies that transform the power of personal branding.

Michelle Obama and Authentic Engagement

Michelle Obama's 'Let's Move' initiative, which was launched with the noble aim of combating childhood obesity, focuses on promoting an active lifestyle and advocating for better nutrition standards. This initiative, coupled with her deeply personal and inspiring memoir, *Becoming*, serve as exemplary demonstrations of the power inherent in authenticity. *Becoming* offers an intimate peering into Obama's life, from her childhood experiences to her years in the White House, allowing readers to connect with her on a deeply personal level.

By sharing genuine personal narratives and championing causes she is passionately committed to, such as healthy living and education for young girls worldwide, Obama has managed to forge deep connections with people across the globe. Her approach goes beyond simple advocacy; it invites her audience into her world, sharing in her challenges and triumphs. This strategy not only fosters a genuine connection with her audience but also significantly bolsters her personal brand. In doing so, it demonstrates how authenticity and passion are not just about maintaining public image but about transforming public perception and exerting influence.

Through her efforts, Obama has shown that being true to oneself and passionately advocating for one's beliefs can have a profound impact, not just on individual lives but on societal norms and values. Her initiatives and personal storytelling exemplify how authenticity and dedication can inspire change and encourage others to take action for a better future.

Melinda Gates and Strategic Advocacy

Melinda Gates' unwavering dedication to philanthropy shines brightly, especially through her impactful work in global health and her tireless pursuit of gender equality. Her actions unveil the transformative power of strategic advocacy coupled with a deep, heartfelt commitment to societal betterment. By focusing her considerable energies and resources on these critical areas, Gates tackles some of the globe's most daunting challenges head-on. In doing so, she not only addresses urgent issues but also solidifies her personal brand as a spotlight of profound influence, boundless compassion, and steadfast dedication to catalyzing positive change in society.

Her approach is a masterclass in how targeted, intentional action can significantly uplift communities and improve lives. Through her initiatives, Gates has made strides in breaking down barriers to healthcare access, enhancing educational opportunities, and empowering women and girls around the world. Her work goes beyond mere philanthropy; it's a blueprint for how dedicated advocacy can lead to substantial advancements in global health and gender equality.

Gates' efforts inspire future leaders. She demonstrates that with determination, a clear vision, and a compassionate heart, it's possible to make a lasting impact on the world. Her legacy is a testament to the idea that when we channel our resources and energy towards the greater good, we can forge a brighter, more equitable future for all. This approach not only sets an inspiring example for others to follow but also shows the importance of leadership in tackling global issues.

Oprah Winfrey and Career Adaptability

Oprah Winfrey's journey showcases a masterful pivot from being a media mogul to a philanthropist and back, all the while maintaining a core message of authenticity, empathy, and empowerment. This trajectory paved the way for the significance of adaptability in shaping one's personal brand. Through her various initiatives, including the influential 'Oprah's Book Club' and the creation of the OWN (Oprah Winfrey Network), she has skillfully leveraged her platform and influence. Her efforts are not just about personal success but are deeply rooted in the desire to make a positive impact on the lives of others. Winfrey's approach, which seamlessly blends entertainment with education and philanthropy, serves as a powerful example of how one can use their influence for the greater good, inspiring countless individuals to strive for personal growth and to help others along their journey.

Her personal brand is a testament to the idea that one's career path may evolve, but core values and passions remain constant. Through her adaptability, Winfrey has built a personal brand that transcends industries, making her an icon of inspiration and authenticity. She shows us that by embracing change and continuously learning, we can create a powerful personal brand that resonates with others.

For the Women at the Helm: Actionable Steps for Immediate Improvement

In a world where first impressions are often digital, understanding how to effectively present and market oneself online is paramount. *It's also not easy.*

To help navigate the challenges of personal branding, here are a few actionable steps for you to take today to improve your digital presence and build an authentic personal brand.

1. **Define Your Personal Brand With Introspection:** Start the journey by delving deep into your own values, beliefs, and strengths. Understanding what you stand for, pinpointing your unique skills, and identifying features that set you apart in your industry are foundational steps. This level of self-awareness is critical for building a personal brand that genuinely represents you and resonates with your target audience.

2. **Audit Your Online Presence:** Undertake a thorough examination of all your social media profiles and any personal websites to ensure they accurately reflect your personal brand and the message you intend to project. Evaluate every piece of information from images to bio descriptions, ensuring consistency and professionalism across all channels. This step is indispensable for cultivating a cohesive and strong personal brand presence

online.

3. **Enhance Your Professional Image:** Dedicate time
   to meticulously update your profiles, photographs,
   biographies, and any content that falls short of
   embodying the personal brand you aspire to portray. This
   may involve professional photoshoots, revising outdated
   content, and aligning all public-facing material with your
   brand's ethos. Such coherence across different media
   enhances the credibility and impact of your brand.

4. **Engage with Your Audience:** Foster a vibrant
   community by engaging in meaningful interactions
   with your followers. Regular, authentic communication
   can turn casual followers into loyal brand advocates,
   significantly extending your brand's influence. Whether
   through comments, direct messages, or shared
   experiences, building relationships is key to community
   engagement.

5. **Share Valuable Content:** Commit yourself to
   consistently produce and share content that not only
   highlights your expertise but also provides genuine value
   to your audience. This could range from educational
   articles, insightful blog posts, engaging videos, to
   interactive live sessions that inform, entertain, or inspire
   your followers. Establishing yourself as a thought leader
   necessitates a strategic approach to content creation.

6. **Network Strategically:** Actively seek out and connect with like-minded individuals and groups that align with your brand values. Networking is not just about expanding your contacts list; it's about building meaningful relationships that can lead to collaborative opportunities, mentorship, and shared growth both in the digital realm and in real life. Attend industry events, join relevant forums, and participate in discussions to enhance your network strategically.

7. **Seek Feedback:** Regularly solicit constructive feedback from your peers, mentors, and audience to gain valuable information into how your personal brand is perceived. Such feedback is a goldmine for identifying areas of improvement, understanding audience needs, and refining your brand strategy. Embrace both positive and negative feedback as opportunities for growth and adaptation.

8. **Seek out Your Mentor:** Identify and approach a mentor who has successfully navigated the path you're on. The right mentor can offer invaluable guidance, support, and encouragement, helping you to navigate the challenges of personal branding with wisdom and grace. A mentor's experience can illuminate your path, providing clarity and direction as you carve out your unique brand identity.

9. **Be Patient:** Recognize that the process of building

a compelling personal brand is a long-term endeavor. It demands patience, persistence, and consistent effort. Progress may be slow at times, but it's important to stay committed to your vision and values. Patience is a virtue in the journey of personal branding, where incremental progress leads to lasting impact.

10. **Remember to Celebrate Your Progress:** Take time to acknowledge and celebrate every achievement along your personal branding journey, no matter how small. Recognizing your accomplishments is not only rewarding but also motivating. It serves as a tangible reminder of your dedication, growth, and the strides you've made towards establishing a strong, authentic personal brand. Celebrations reinforce your commitment and inspire continued effort towards your goals.

By diligently expanding on these foundational steps, you have the opportunity to cultivate a personal brand that not only distinguishes itself in a crowded marketplace but also maintains a sense of authenticity and serves as a source of inspiration to others.

10

The Journey Ahead

Reflecting on this Journey

We've embarked on an extensive exploration through the rich and multifaceted landscape of branding, meticulously uncovering the various layers that render it a complex yet utterly rewarding challenge. This journey has transcended the conventional boundaries of marketing, evolving into a profound exploration of authenticity's essence. It's been about diving deep into the art of storytelling, crafting narratives that not only resonate with audiences but also reflect the genuine spirit of the brand. Along the way, we've learned the importance of building communities, fostering a sense of belonging and connection among individuals who share common values and visions. This adventure has been about innovation—finding unique, creative ways to express our brand's identity while remaining steadfast to our core values. Through this process, we've gained invaluable discovery into the power of branding, not just as a tool for business, but as a means to make meaningful impacts in the world.

The Unique Strengths of Women in Branding

The branding process undergoes a profound transformation when infused with the unique strengths and perspectives that women bring to the table. Our inherent capacity for empathy, a trait deeply rooted in our ability to understand and share the feelings of others, allows us to connect with audiences on a far more profound level. This is not just about recognizing what people want or need; it's about comprehending their hopes, fears, and dreams, enabling us to craft messages that resonate on a deeply personal level, far beyond mere transactional interactions.

Our intuitive grasp of community dynamics is another superpower in the realm of branding. This skill enables us to cultivate an environment where customers feel they belong, a place that echoes their values and aspirations. By doing so, we turn casual customers into loyal advocates who feel a strong, personal connection to the brand. This sense of belonging is invaluable, as it fosters a vibrant community around our brands, making every member an integral part of our ongoing narrative.

In addition to these qualities, our innate creativity plays a pivotal role in how we present and evolve brands. This creativity isn't confined to aesthetics or superficial embellishments. Instead, it's about thinking outside the conventional boundaries to solve problems, innovate, and present brands in ways that captivate and engage. Our creative approach is holistic, considering every facet of the brand experience to ensure it's not only visually appealing but also meaningful and impactful.

These attributes, among others, empower us as women to create brands that do far more than merely sell products. They allow us to forge deep, lasting bonds with consumers, resonating on an emotional level that transcends the traditional seller-buyer dynamic. Through our unique contributions, we're able to breathe life into brands, transforming them into living entities that communicate, connect, and grow with their audiences. This is the essence of modern branding, and it's an area where the contributions of women are not only invaluable but absolutely indispensable.

The Power of Authenticity in Branding

Our journey embarked from a foundational principle that stands paramount—authenticity. In a world awash with an endless sea of messages, all clamoring for the spotlight of our attention, the act of authenticity shines the brightest, guiding customers to our shores like a lighthouse in the dark. It transcends mere genuineness; it embodies the essence of being unapologetically true to our core beliefs and values. By steadfastly adhering to this principle, we can create a brand that doesn't just mimic the superficial trends of the day but is a genuine reflection of our deeply held values, mission, and vision. This commitment to authenticity ensures that every interaction, every product, and every message we send resonates with the truth of who we are, establishing a profound and meaningful connection with our audience.

Embracing the Art of Storytelling

Storytelling is undeniably the soul of any brand. It represents the crucial mechanism through which we connect on a deeply human level, effectively bridging the vast gap that often exists between business and emotion, product and personal experience. It's not merely about the narrative; it's about creating a resonant experience that touches the hearts and minds of the audience. Good stories do much more than facilitate transactions; they have the power to transform customers into a deeply loyal audience, one that is not just passively consuming but actively engaged and eagerly awaiting the next chapter that we, as creators, marketers, or entrepreneurs, will write together. This dynamic process of storytelling is not just about selling a product or a service; it's about crafting an ongoing relationship that is built on a foundation of trust, shared values, and mutual respect.

Building Community and Fostering Loyalty

Community is undoubtedly the foundation of enduring success. It's the magical place where simple engagement blossoms into a deep sense of belonging, and where ordinary customers evolve into passionate advocates for the brand. This transformation is largely driven by key elements such as mentorship, which offers guidance and support; collaboration, which brings diverse ideas and talents together; and shared values, which create a strong, united vision. Through our experiences, we've witnessed firsthand the power of communities. They thrive on mutual support and understanding, fostering a loyalty that goes far beyond the traditional customer-brand relationship. In these communities, members not only share resources and knowledge but also celebrate each other's successes, creating a nurturing environment that propels everyone forward.

Navigating Innovation and Adaptation

The business landscape is perpetually in a state of flux, presenting continuous challenges that compel us to remain agile and drive us towards relentless innovation. In this dynamic and ever-evolving environment, the ability to stay adaptable, to embrace the process of evolution, all while steadfastly clinging to our core values and principles, becomes paramount in securing a competitive edge. This strategy necessitates not only strategic foresight and planning but also a profound commitment to our vision amidst the swirling winds of change.

The remarkable narratives of women who excel by leading with such adaptive innovation stand out as particularly inspiring. These leaders illuminate the path for maintaining a sense of dynamism in our strategies and perspectives, urging us to meet change head-on with resilience, foresight, and an unwavering spirit of perseverance. Through their journeys, we are shown the essence of flexibility, creativity, and an unyielding pursuit of excellence. These stories provide rich, instructive examples that relay the importance of these qualities, teaching us invaluable lessons on how to adeptly navigate the complexities and intricacies of the modern business world.

Indeed, the experiences of these pioneering women stress a broader lesson for all of us in the business community: that success in a rapidly changing global market requires more than just keeping pace with technological advancements and market trends. It demands an intrinsic ability to foresee changes, to innovate continuously, and to adapt strategies in real-time while never losing sight of the enduring principles that define our missions and visions. By embodying these ideals, we can aspire to not just survive but thrive in this challenging, yet exciting business landscape.

Envisioning the Future: A New Era of Branding

Looking forward, I envision a branding landscape that is utterly transformed by the insights and principles we've explored together. Imagine a world where the cornerstones of branding—authenticity, storytelling, community engagement, innovation, and the distinctive contributions of women—are not merely appreciated but are deemed essential for achievement and success. This is a future brimming with vibrant possibilities, a future where brands transcend the traditional confines of marketing to do more than just sell something. They inspire, they empower, and they forge deep, lasting connections with their audience, creating a profound impact on society.

In this envisioned future, every brand has a story that resonates on a personal level, every message is crafted with genuine intent and deep understanding, and every marketing effort is meticulously designed to cultivate meaningful relationships and conversations. Here, storytelling becomes an art form, a means for brands to communicate their values and missions in ways that touch the hearts and minds of consumers, making them feel part of something larger than themselves.

This future is one where diversity and inclusion are not buzzwords or afterthoughts but are embedded in the very fabric of brand identity. They drive creativity and innovation, pushing boundaries

and opening doors to new ideas and perspectives. Brands in this
future are celebrated not just for their products or services but for
their role in shaping a more inclusive society, one *where every voice
is heard and valued.*

It's a future where technology and human creativity intersect
in the most enriching ways, enabling brands to reach out and
connect with people across the globe in personalized ways. Digital
platforms and social media evolve to become spaces of genuine
interaction, meaningful conversations, where communities are
built and nurtured, and where brands can truly make a difference
in the lives of those that rely on them.

In this future, the success of a brand is measured not just
by its financial achievements but by the impact it has on its
community and the world at large. Brands that understand
the importance of their role in society and act responsibly and
ethically will thrive. This is a future filled with opportunities for
brands that dare to dream big, to innovate, and to embrace the
principles of authenticity, storytelling, community engagement,
and diversity. It's a future we can all look forward to, one where the
branding landscape is not only transformed but elevated to heights
previously unimagined.

Call to Action: Embrace Authenticity in Your Branding Endeavors

As we set sail on this exhilarating journey towards a future filled with boundless opportunities and collaborative successes, I want to emphasize the paramount importance of holding the torch of authenticity, higher than any other virtue. It is absolutely essential to imbue every facet of your branding endeavors with the essence of your true self, alongside the ambitious objectives you strive to realize. Remember, the goal surpasses the simple transactional exchanges of selling a product or service. It's about meticulously sculpting a legacy that resonates with undeniable elements of truth, true inner beauty, and a deep, overarching sense of purpose.

This meticulous approach to branding, grounded in authenticity, will set you distinctly apart in the teeming marketplace. More importantly, it will enable you to forge a profound and enduring connection with your audience. This isn't just about making an impression; it's about establishing a bedrock of trust and admiration that will stand the test of time. By doing so, you're not just selling a product or service; you're inviting your audience into a world that's compelling, resonant, and inherently truthful. This methodology will not only captivate their minds but will also win their hearts, ensuring your brand becomes an integral and cherished part of their lives, just as it has become for you.

Benefits for you, the Reader

Stronger Leadership: Demonstrating empathy and authenticity in leadership not only inspires trust but also fosters a sense of cohesion among team members. By genuinely understanding and caring for their team's well-being, leaders can create a supportive atmosphere that encourages openness and collaboration. This approach enables leaders to effectively guide their teams through challenges, creating a strong, united front that is capable of achieving remarkable results. Empathetic leadership encourages team members to develop their own leadership skills, contributing to the overall growth and success of the organization.

—**Authentic Personal Branding**: In today's highly competitive landscape, crafting an honest professional narrative is more important than ever. It enhances one's relatability and attractiveness to both clients and colleagues alike, setting the foundation for genuine, lasting relationships that are based on trust and mutual respect. This authenticity makes individuals stand out, enabling them to connect with their audience on a deeper level, which is crucial for building a strong, personal brand that resonates with people and remains memorable over time.

—**Deeper Connections**: A culture of openness encourages reciprocity among business partners, paving the way for more meaningful and beneficial business relationships. This level of transparency is the cornerstone of building a network that's both supportive and enduring. By fostering an environment where partners feel comfortable sharing successes and challenges, organizations can discover opportunities for collaboration that leverage each party's strengths, leading to mutually beneficial outcomes and a stronger, more connected industry ecosystem.

—**Enhanced Problem-Solving**: Cultivating an environment where challenges and issues are shared openly leads to the generation of innovative solutions. When team members feel safe to express their concerns and ideas, the collective brainpower can tackle problems from multiple angles, often leading to breakthroughs that wouldn't be possible in a more restrictive environment. This collaborative approach to problem-solving not only accelerates the resolution process but also inspires creativity and innovation, ensuring the team remains agile and capable of overcoming future obstacles.

—**Personal and Professional Growth**: Encountering and overcoming vulnerabilities not only builds character but also fosters resilience and adaptability. This growth mindset is invaluable in both personal development and professional advancement, as it prepares individuals to face future challenges with confidence and agility. By embracing challenges as opportunities for growth, individuals can push beyond their comfort zones, leading to personal breakthroughs and professional achievements. This continuous cycle of learning and adaptation is key to thriving in today's fast-paced world, making personal and professional growth an ongoing journey rather than a distant goal.

Final Thoughts: Maya Angelou's Wisdom and the Journey

Reflecting upon the profound wisdom of Maya Angelou offers us a guiding light for our journey ahead. Her exploration reminds us that it's not merely our achievements, but the impact we make, the emotions we stir, and the lasting memories we forge that will truly define our measure of success. In my personal journey of branding, I've learned to embrace vulnerability not as a weakness, but as a formidable strength. By intricately weaving my personal narrative into the very fabric of my own brand, I've discovered the unparalleled value of authenticity. I've found that the most powerful and enduring connections are those that are nurtured from a place of genuine compassion and empathy, resonating directly from the heart. This approach has not only transformed how I view my brand but has also deeply influenced the way I engage with my audience, fostering a community built on trust and mutual respect.

As we close this book together, I'm filled with gratitude for the companionship on this journey. The path ahead is bright with the promise of innovation, collaboration, and transformation. Together, we can redefine the future of women in the professional landscape, leveraging our collective strength, wisdom, and creativity.

Thank you for joining me on this incredible adventure. The road doesn't end here; it's merely the beginning of a new chapter in the quest to **Brand Like A Girl**.

Appendix A: Recommended Readings and Resources

Personal Branding

- *You Are a Brand!* by Catherine Kaputa - A great start to understanding how personal branding works and how to leverage it for your success.

- *Branding Yourself* by Erik Deckers and Kyle Lacy - Practical advice for using social media and other online tools to create a powerful personal online presence.

- Online Resource: I offer custom programs and additional guidance to Branding Like A Girl and other self-marketing help on my website: www.julie-adams.com

Leadership

- *Lean In: Women, Work, and the Will to Lead* by Sheryl Sandberg - An essential read for women looking to climb the ladder of leadership and make a significant impact.

- *Dare to Lead* by Brené Brown - Focusing on vulnerability and courage in leadership, this book offers invaluable insights into what makes a great leader.

Marketing

- *This Is Marketing* by Seth Godin - Reimagines marketing as empathy and service, offering timeless advice for connecting with your audience authentically.

- *Made to Stick* by Chip Heath and Dan Heath - explores why some ideas thrive while others die, providing a crucial understanding of how to make your brand's message stick.

Resources

Below is a list of further resources for exploring this topic, including books, articles, and organizations dedicated to supporting women in business. These valuable tools offer additional insights, strategies, and communities that can empower readers on their own journeys to break barriers.

Remember, you are not alone in this journey. Let's continue to support and uplift one another as we strive for progress and equality in the business world. Together, we can make a real difference.

1) Sandberg, S (2013). Lean In: Women, Work, and the Will to Lead. New York: Knopf.

2) Grant, S (2017). Option B: Facing Adversity, Building Resilience, and Finding Joy. New York: Knopf.

3) Brown, B (2010). The Gifts of Imperfection: Let Go of Who You Think You're Supposed to Be and Embrace Who You Are. Hazelden Publishing.

4) Audrey Hepburn Children's Fund. (n.d.). Retrieved from https://www.audreyhepburn.com/about/the-childrens-fund/

5) UNICEF USA. (n.d.). Retrieved from https://www.unicefusa.org/mission

6) Save the Children. (n.d.). Retrieved from https://www.savethechildren.org/us/what-we-do

7) Women's Leadership Institute: https://womensleadershipinstitute.org/

8) National Association for Female Executives: https://www.nafe.com/

9) The Glass Hammer: http://theglass

10) Biden/Harris Campaign: https://joebiden.com/kamala-harris/

11) Kamala Harris' acceptance speech: https://www.cnn.com/videos/politics/2020/08/20/full-speech-kamala-harris-vice-president-democratic-national-convention-vpx.cnn

Additional Resources

Forbes Women: https://www.forbes.com/women

Lean In Community: https://leanin.org/

National Association of Women Business Owners:
https://www.nawbo.org/

TED Talks:
https://www.ted.com/topics/women+in+business

Appendix B: Glossary

This section offers definitions for key terms and concepts discussed throughout *Brand Like A Girl*, serving as a quick-reference tool for readers. Some of the terms included are:

—**Brand Equity:** The value that a brand adds to a product or service, distinguishing it from competitors and building customer loyalty.

—**Competitor Analysis:** An evaluation of the strengths and weaknesses of a brand's competitors to determine how it can gain a competitive advantage.

—**Content Marketing:** A strategic marketing approach focused on creating and distributing valuable, relevant, and consistent content to attract and retain a clearly defined audience.

—**Personal Branding:** The practice of marketing people and their careers as brands, highlighting individual skills, personality, and expertise.

—**SEO (Search Engine Optimization):** The process of optimizing online content so that a search engine likes to show it as a top result for searches of a certain keyword.

—**SWOT Analysis:** A strategic planning technique used to help identify Strengths, Weaknesses, Opportunities, and Threats related to business competition or project planning.

—**Target Audience:** The specific group of people that a brand aims to reach with its products or services.

Appendix C: Call to Action

Join the Brand Like A Girl Community: Let's take your brand to new heights together. When you become a part of the Brand Like A Girl Community, you're not just joining a group; you're stepping into a powerful circle dedicated to elevating your brand. Here's what awaits you:

Exclusive Mentorship: One-on-one sessions with the author tailored specifically to your brand's needs. Transformative advice and strategies to take your brand from good to unforgettable.

Premium Resources: Access in-depth materials and guides not available to the general public. Further your strategy and learning with these high-quality resources.

Networking Opportunities: Connect with other ambitious professionals in a variety of industries. Grow your network and find potential collaborators or mentors.

Direct Implementation Support: Get hands-on assistance in implementing the strategies and insights from the book into your own brand's practices.

How to Join: Interested in elevating your brand with personalized mentorship and exclusive resources? Go to www.brandlikeagirl.com to learn more about the benefits of joining the Brand Like A Girl Community and how to sign up.

By investing in your brand's success through mentorship and continuous learning, you're setting the stage for unparalleled growth and influence in your industry.

About the Author

Julie is a seasoned marketing professional with over a decade of experience transforming challenges into successes and propelling startups into thriving businesses. Her career is marked by impactful collaborations with entrepreneurs, global brands, and even political and celebrity figures. Julie specializes in developing tailored brand and marketing strategies that not only deliver measurable results but also create a lasting impact. She has earned a reputation as the go-to strategist for businesses ready to make a meaningful difference.

Julie possesses a deep understanding of the unique challenges and opportunities faced by female-led businesses. With her expertise, she crafts strategies that build brands capable of connecting, resonating, and thriving in competitive markets. Beyond her professional achievements, Julie is a passionate advocate for inclusive business practices. Her commitment is reflected in her work with organizations such as the NSBA Leadership Council and the American Marketing Association, where she champions meaningful change through legislation and education.

Holding degrees in Mass Communications/Public Relations and Marketing, coupled with hands-on experience founding multiple businesses, Julie skillfully combines theoretical knowledge with practical application. Her entrepreneurial spirit and strategic vision are central to her work, driving brands to reach unprecedented success.

The Inspiration Behind Brand Like A Girl

Drawing from a wellspring of personal insight and industry experience, Julie set pen to paper to compose *Brand Like A Girl*. In essence, *Brand Like A Girl* is more than just a book—it's a movement. Julie's labor of love is designed to inspire, guide, and celebrate the burgeoning tribe of female marketers and entrepreneurs ready to carve their niche in the business world with authenticity, ingenuity, and perseverance. Her motivation was multifaceted:

—**Market Evolution:** Julie recognized early on the shifting paradigms with female consumers gaining unprecedented influence and the consequent need for marketing strategies that resonate on a more personalized level.

—**Industry Gap:** Striking disparities in resources for female-led initiatives in the branding sphere prompted Julie to address this void. Her aim? To create a repository of wisdom that acknowledges and amplifies the essence of female entrepreneurship.

—**Empowerment Through Knowledge:** At the core of her vision was a fierce ambition to empower women. By weaving together lessons from her personal journeys and distilled wisdom from her professional engagements, Julie aspired to craft a manual that would act as a compass for women navigating the tempests of the market.

—**Practical Wisdom:** With *Brand Like A Girl*, Julie bridges theoretical knowledge and experience with actionable insights. The book is studded with real-life case studies and scenarios that not only illuminate the path forward but also ensure readers are well-equipped to tread it boldly.

www.ingramcontent.com/pod-product-compliance
Lightning Source LLC
Chambersburg PA
CBHW060923120626
46557CB00003B/855